Office XP Integration

PROJECT 1

Integrating Office XP Applications and the World Wide Web

OBJECTIVES

You will have mastered the material in this project when you can:

- Integrate the Office XP applications to create a Web site
- Add hyperlinks to a Word document
- Embed an Excel chart into a Word document
- Add scrolling text to a Web page created in Word
- Add a hyperlink to a PowerPoint slide
- Create Web pages from a PowerPoint presentation
- Create a data access page from an Access database

A Little Rest and Relaxation

and Amazing Things Happen

Travel brochures entice and invite you to experience exotic locales that can improve your state of mind. Vacations help to eliminate daily stresses, offer opportunities to spend quality time with family and friends, and provide exercise in the great outdoors. Holiday packages are plentiful if you want to explore destination possibilities.

Maybe you are feeling tired and desire a little rest and relaxation away from it all, a haven where you can recapture your spirit in comfort and peace. There you find friendly staff to attend to your every need, nutritious meals, breathtaking views of Chicago's skyline from clean, private rooms tastefully decorated with soothing artwork to promote the healing process. Is this a weekend retreat? you ask. No, this is Chicago's Northwestern Memorial Hospital's Feinberg Inpatient Pavilion, designed with patients' needs in mind.

The hospital's advertising slogan, Making Amazing Things Happen, applied to the efforts of the 4,500 employees, 1,000 physicians, and 800 volunteers involved in planning the state-of-the-art building for more than a decade. The design team formed 125 user groups composed of staff, patients, and their families to develop an ideal patient encounter. They provided input on designing areas that facilitate communication

and ergonomics and even staged a mock cardiac arrest to develop optimal working conditions.

The $580 million medical center opened in 1999 and contains the floor area of 44 football fields. Intertwined in this space are 600 miles of fiber-optic and high-speed copper cable that integrate computer functions. Patients are introduced to the innovative computerization techniques the minute they enter the medical center. Instead of registering at a central desk, they proceed directly to a nursing unit on a particular floor. Once the patients are settled in their beds, caregivers complete their registration forms by inputting personal data in notebook computers that are connected to the hospital's computer system through data connections in each private room.

Various medical personnel then can access this data. Doctors use notebook computers to retrieve the records as they make their rounds. Caregivers in the emergency room can retrieve laboratory reports seconds after the tests are complete, which enhances their ability to treat critical patients when seconds matter most. Billing department employees can generate comprehensive statements that detail specific procedures and charges. Students throughout the world can view the latest surgical procedures via teleconferences made possible by special cameras in each operating room.

Another aspect of computer integration throughout the hospital is the use of filmless X-rays. Instead of using the traditional method of exposing and then developing celluloid film, radiology technicians now use the picture archiving and communication system (PACS) to take a digital image. Each of the thousands of X-rays taken monthly is stored on an optical storage system, which eliminates the need to save physical hard copy film in a special room. Caregivers can retrieve these radiology images from workstations throughout the hospital, including intensive care units and the emergency room. When necessary, these files can be transmitted to other medical facilities throughout the world via the Internet.

Northwestern Memorial Hospital integrates its computer applications to maximize patient convenience and minimize costs.

Similarly, in this project, you will utilize the integration features of the Microsoft Office XP applications. Using information already available to you in Word, Excel, Access, and PowerPoint, you will develop a Web site for Garden National Bank as a means for the bank to implement a marketing strategy advertising its benefits and services. This seamless integration makes amazing things happened.

Office XP Integration

PROJECT 1

Integrating Office XP Applications and the World Wide Web

CASE PERSPECTIVE

Garden National Bank is a community bank managed by Liza Oei. In the past, the bank enjoyed great success by being the only bank in its part of town. Recently, the bank's clientele has been using newer services, such as Internet stock brokers and other local financial service providers.

Liza believes that the bank's business would increase if she implements a marketing strategy that advertises the advantages Garden National Bank has over competitors' services. Garden National Bank offers nationally competitive interest rates and savings plans. In addition, Liza employs highly trained financial advisors and a friendly staff. She is investigating ways to advertise these benefits in an efficient and cost-effective way. She thinks a Web site would be the answer, but she is inexperienced with the Internet. Liza knows that you are studying computer technology and asks you to help her create a Web site advertising Garden National Bank.

Introduction

From your meeting with Liza Oei, you were given four files of information to use to create the Web site for Garden National Bank.

1. A Word document that contains the company logo images and company name (Figure 1-1a on page I 1.06).
2. An Excel workbook with a Bar chart graphically illustrating the bank's breakdown of investments by savings product used by customers (Figure 1-1b on page I 1.06).
3. A PowerPoint slideshow that contains general information about the bank (Figure 1-1g on page I 1.07).
4. An Access database that contains savings product information (Figure 1-1c on page I 1.06).

The Garden National Bank Web site should include the following:

1. A home page with a Bar chart that contains the total asset value per savings product (Figure 1-1e on page I 1.07). Three hypertext links also are included on the home page: About Us, Savings Products, and E-mail Comments.
2. The Savings Products data access Web page (Figure 1-1d on page I 1.06) is created from the Access file. Clicking the Savings Products link on the home page accesses this Web page. On this Web page, visitors can scroll through the savings products, categorized by product category.
3. The PowerPoint Web page (Figure 1-1g on page I 1.07) displays information about the bank. Clicking the About Us link on the home page accesses this Web page.
4. Using the E-mail Comments hyperlink, you can create an e-mail message (Figure 1-1f on page I 1.07). E-mail is sent to the e-mail address `manager@isp.com`.

Integration Project — Garden National Bank Web Site

Many businesses today advertise their products and services on the Internet, as described in the Case Perspective. Companies find it easy to create Web pages using information already saved in spreadsheet, database, or presentation software formats. The Web page creation capabilities of Microsoft Office XP make it simple for you to create an entire Web site using the information available. In Word, a document can be created and saved as a Web page. PowerPoint provides the same capability and adds a navigation structure for browsing. In addition, Access provides a Wizard to create data access pages that enable the Web page visitor to navigate through the database.

The following pages contain a detailed explanation of these tasks.

Adding Hyperlinks to a Word Document

The Web site created for Garden National Bank consists of an initial Web page, called the **home page**, with two hyperlinks to other Web pages, an e-mail link, and a Bar chart. Clicking a **hyperlink**, which can be text or an image, allows you to jump to another location. Text is used (About Us, Savings Products, E-mail Comments) for the three hyperlinks on the Garden National Bank home page (Figure 1-1e on page 1.07). The first hyperlink (About Us) jumps to a PowerPoint Web page that contains staff listings and general information about the bank and its products. A second hyperlink (Savings Products) jumps to a data access page that provides inquiry capabilities for customers to access the Garden National Bank's savings product database. This Web page allows inquiries only; updating the database is prohibited. The third hyperlink (E-mail Comments) creates an e-mail message. In order to place the three hyperlinks to the left of the Bar chart, a table will be created in the Word document.

> **More About**
>
> **Web Pages**
>
> Making information available on the Internet is a key aspect of business today. To facilitate this trend, the Office XP applications easily allow you to generate Web pages from existing files. An entire Web site can be created with files from Word, Excel, PowerPoint, or Access, using the Save as Web Page command on the File menu.

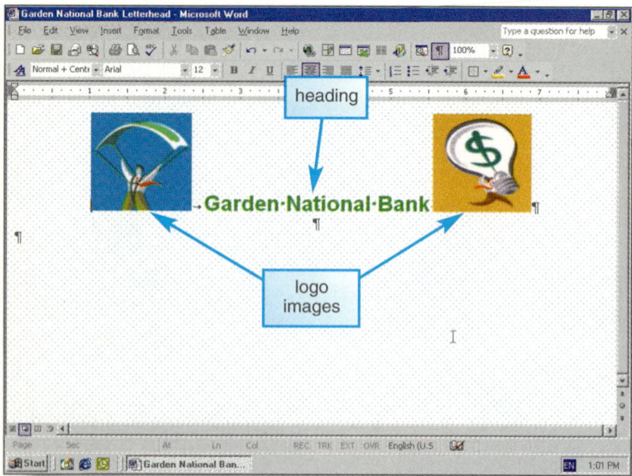

(a) Word Document

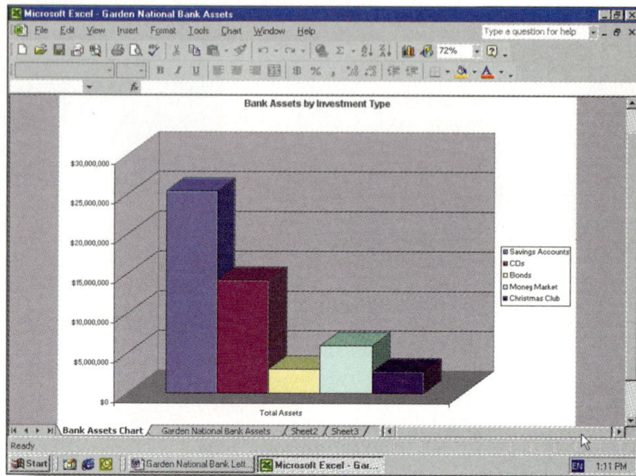

(b) Bar Chart in Excel

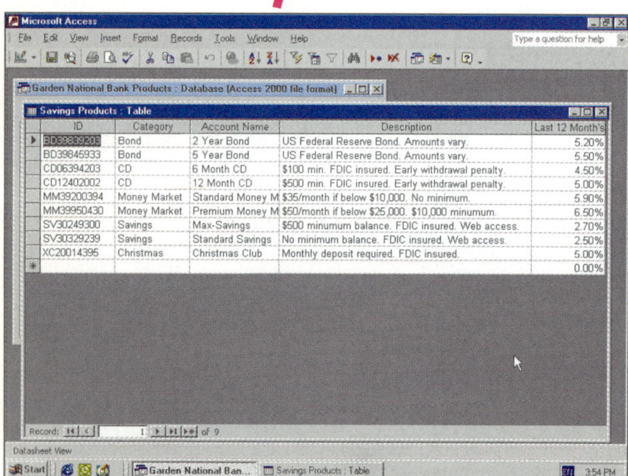

(c) Access Table

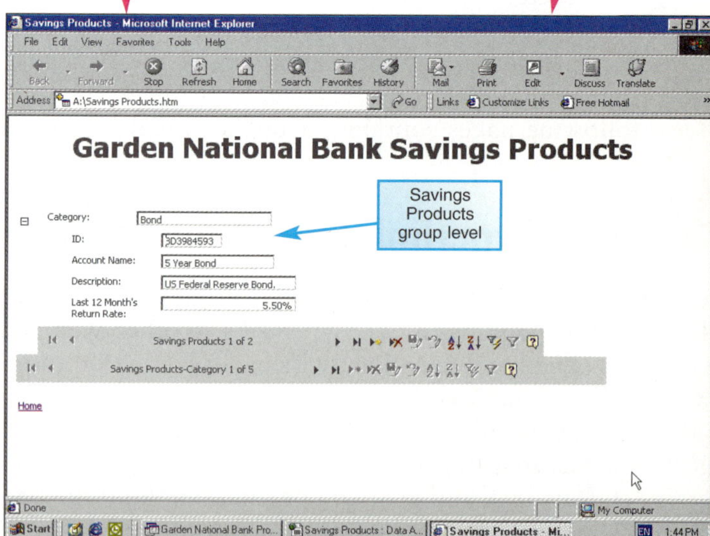

(d) Data Access Page

FIGURE 1-1

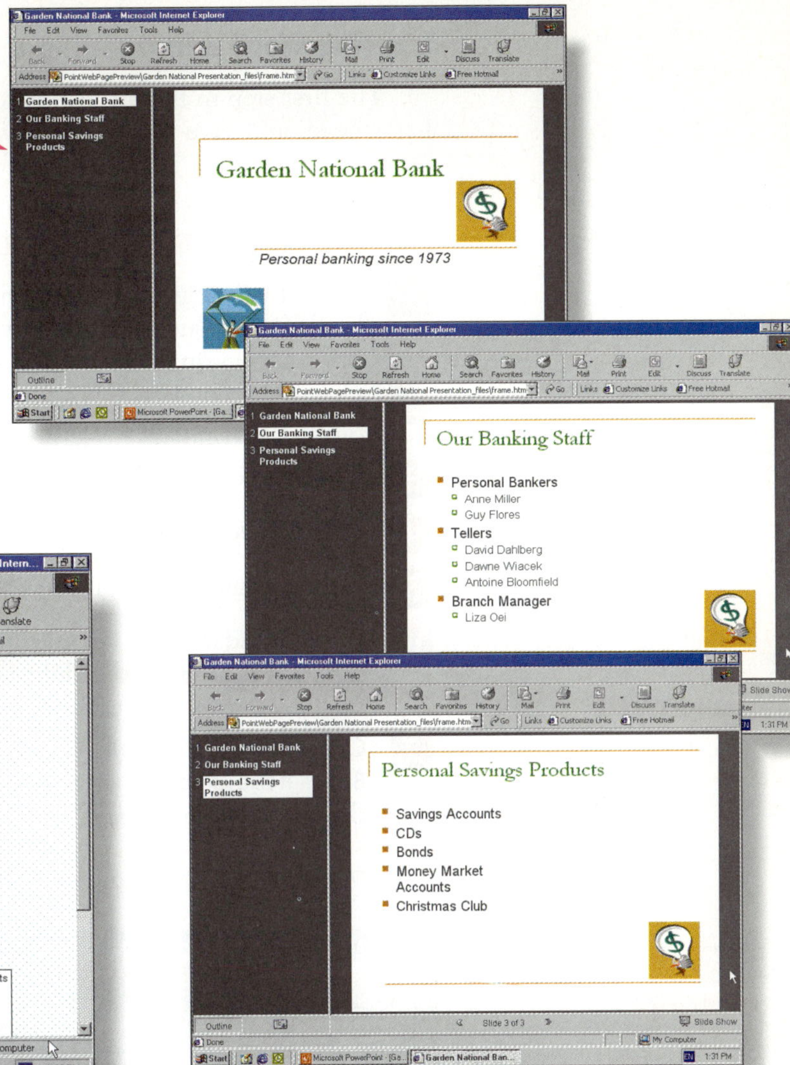

(g) PowerPoint Presentation Saved as Web Pages

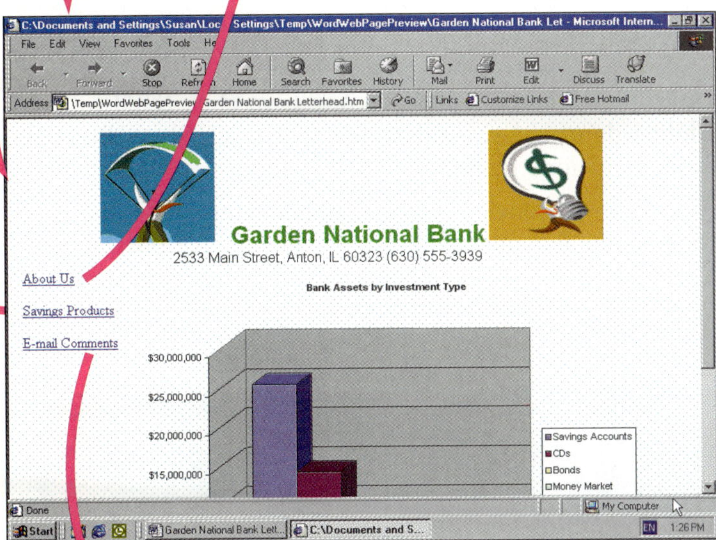

(e) Word Document Saved as a Web Page

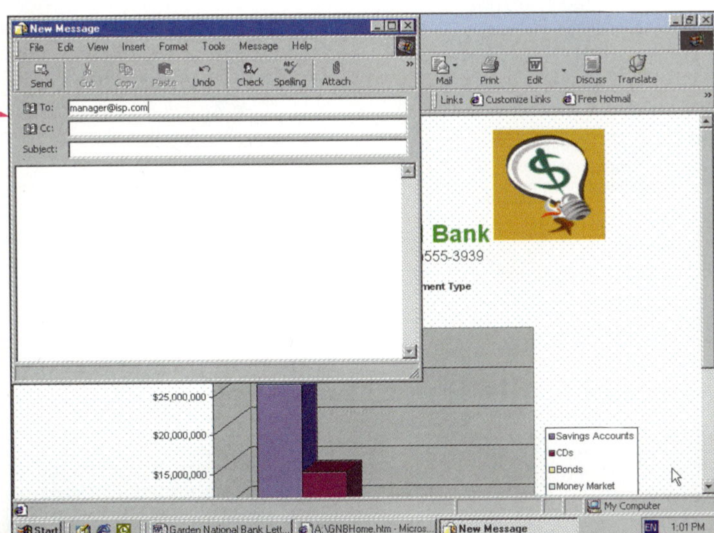

(f) New E-Mail Message Created from Hyperlink

Starting Word and Opening a Document

The first step in this project is to open the Word document, Garden National Bank Letterhead, and save it with the new file name, Garden National Bank Home Page.

TO START WORD, CUSTOMIZE WORD, OPEN AN EXISTING DOCUMENT, AND SAVE THE DOCUMENT WITH ANOTHER NAME

1. Insert the Integration Data Disk in drive A. See the inside back cover of this book for instructions for downloading the Data Disk or see your instructor for information on accessing the files required in this book.
2. Click the Start button on the Windows taskbar. Click Open Office Document on the Start menu.
3. Click the Look in box arrow and then click 3½ Floppy (A:) in the Look in list.
4. Double-click Garden National Bank Letterhead.
5. If the Language bar displays, click its Minimize button.
6. If the Standard and Formatting toolbars display on one row, click the Toolbar Options button on the right side of either toolbar and then click Show Buttons on Two Rows on the Toobar Options menu.
7. Click File on the menu bar and then click Save As. Type `Garden National Bank Home Page` in the File name text box and then click the Save button in the Save As dialog box.

The document is saved as Garden National Bank Home Page (Figure 1-2).

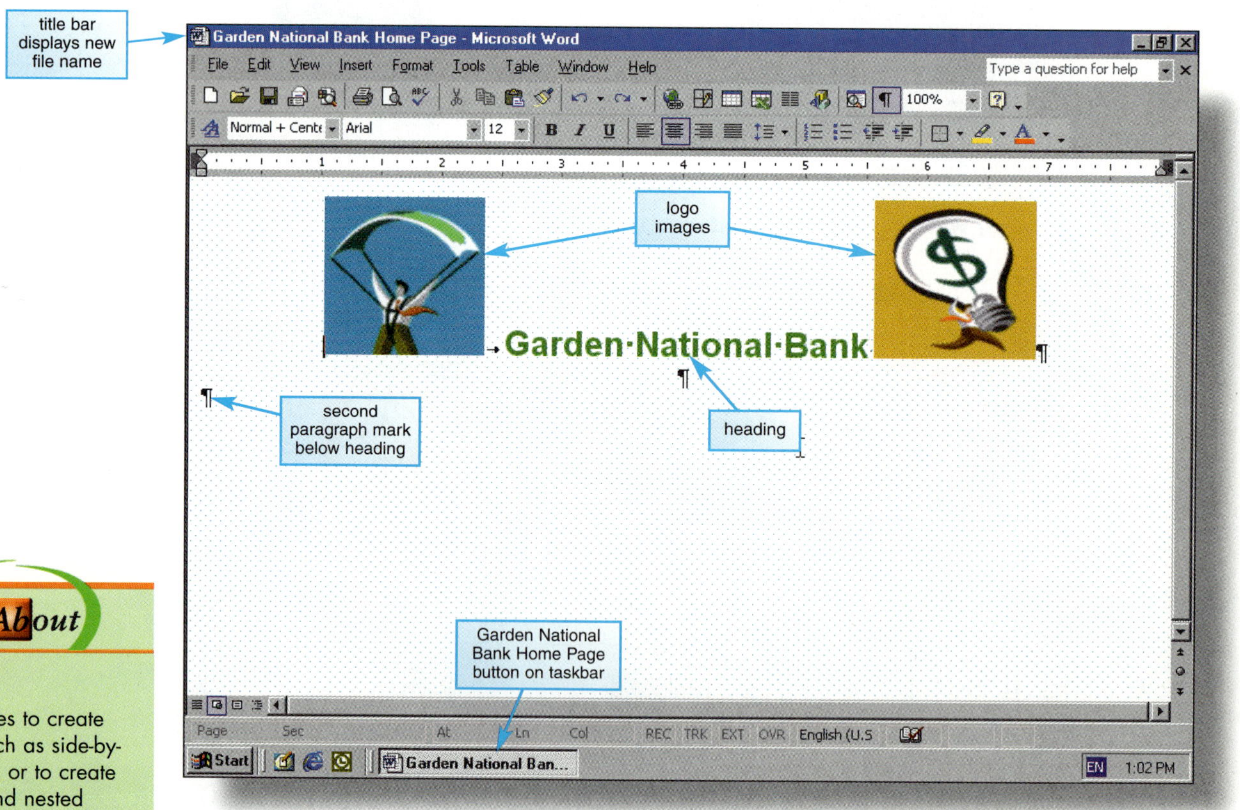

FIGURE 1-2

More About

Tables

You can use tables to create page layouts, such as side-by-side paragraphs, or to create text, graphics, and nested tables on a Web page. Tables are used frequently in Web pages to structure information and images.

Inserting a Table into a Word Document

The next step is to insert a table with two columns and one row. The left column will contain three hyperlinks. The right column will contain the Bar chart.

Perform the following steps to add a table to the Garden National Bank Home Page document.

Steps To Insert a Table into a Word Document

1 Position the insertion point on the second paragraph mark after the heading Garden National Bank. Click Table on the menu bar, point to Insert, and then click Table.

The Insert Table dialog box displays (Figure 1-3).

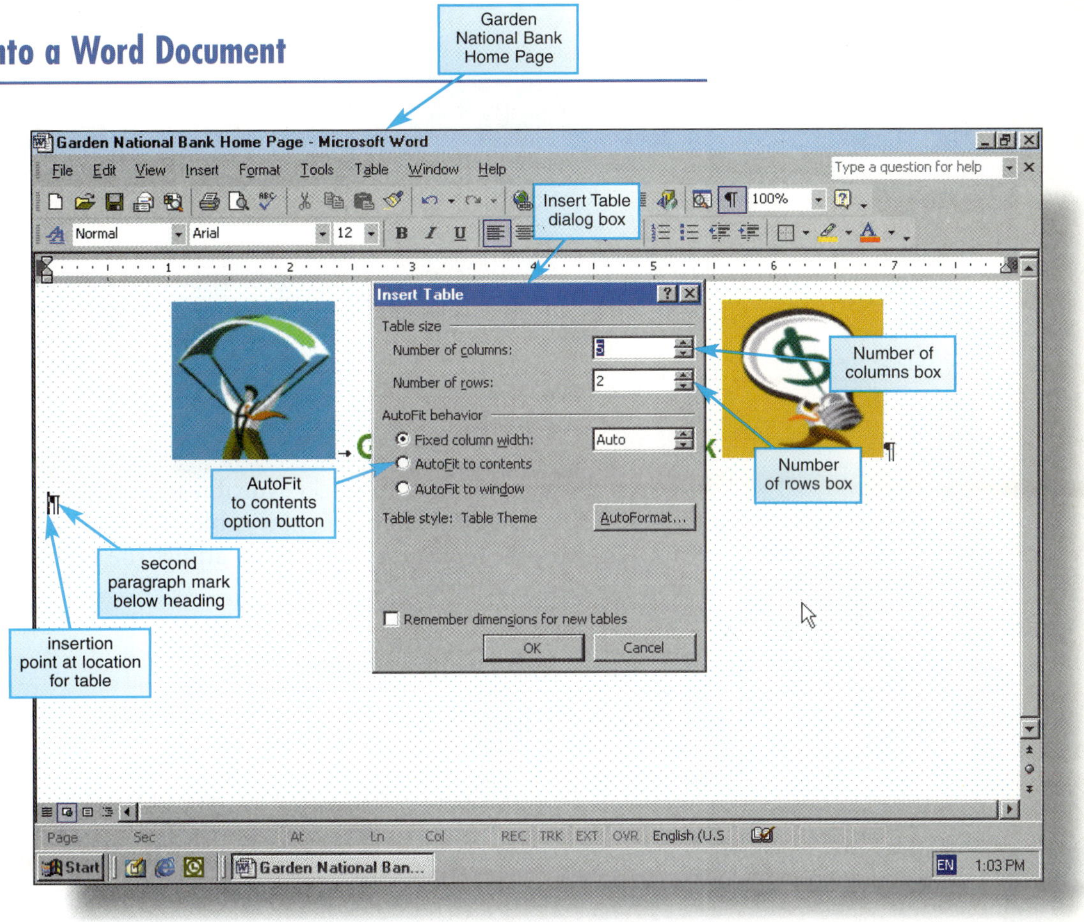

FIGURE 1-3

2 Type 2 in the Number of columns box and then press the TAB key. Type 1 in the Number of rows box and then click AutoFit to contents in the AutoFit behavior area. Point to the OK button.

The new settings display in the Insert Table dialog box (Figure 1-4).

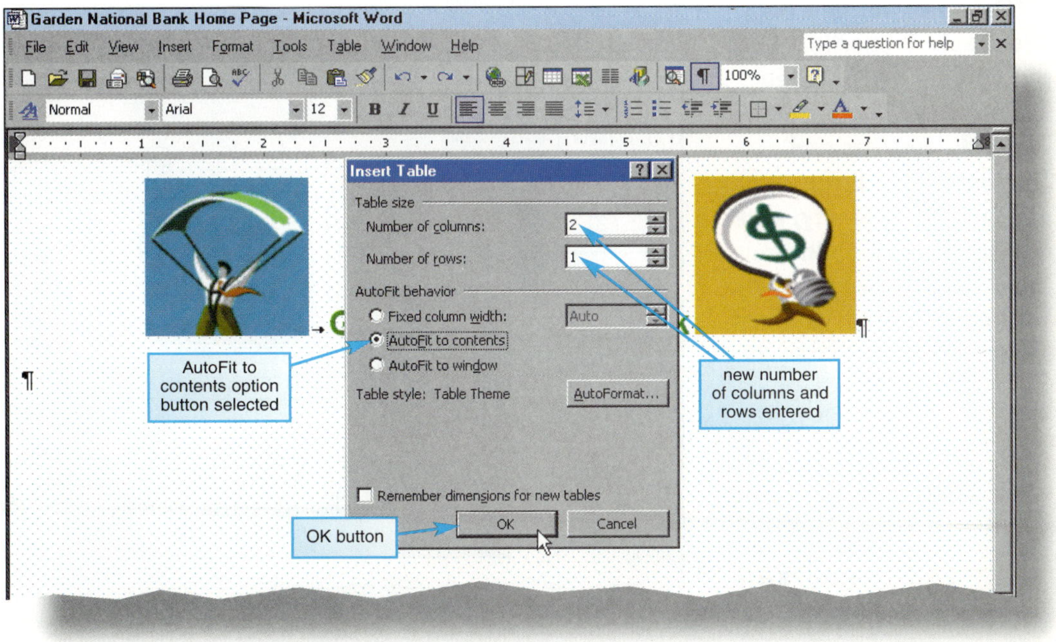

FIGURE 1-4

3 **Click the OK button.**

The table displays in the Word document (Figure 1-5).

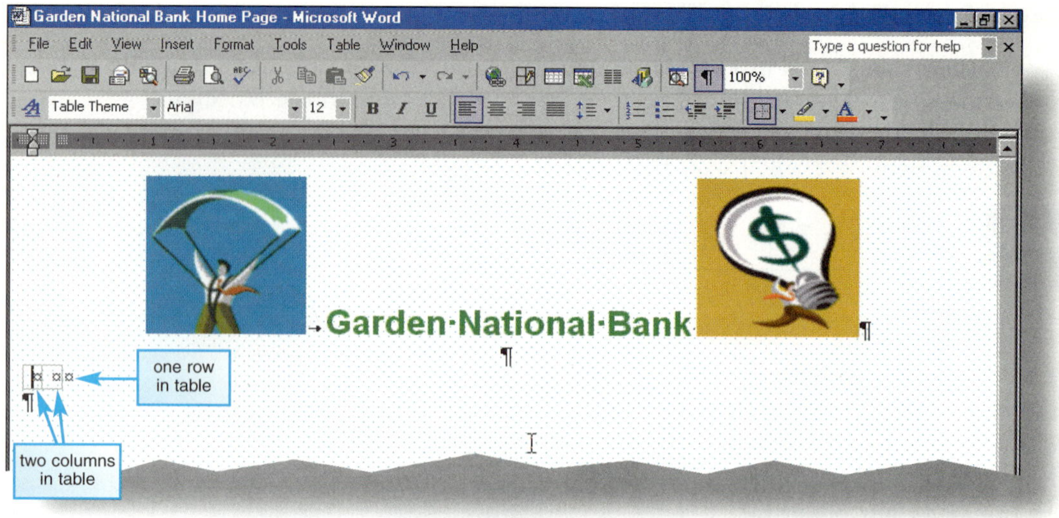

FIGURE 1-5

Other Ways

1. Click Insert Table button on Standard toolbar, drag through one row and two columns, click mouse button
2. In Voice Command mode say, "Insert Table," [drag through one row and two columns, click mouse button]

Step 2 instructed you to select AutoFit to contents. The **AutoFit to contents** option allows you to make the columns in a table automatically fit the contents. If you do not select AutoFit to contents, you can adjust the column widths manually using the sizing handles.

Eliminating the Table Border

The two-column, one-row table has been inserted into the Word document. The table border is not necessary for the Web page. The next steps instruct you on how to remove the border of the table.

Steps To Remove the Table Border

1 **Click Table on the menu bar and then click Table Properties. Click the Borders and Shading button in the Table sheet. When the Borders and Shading dialog box displays, if necessary, click the Borders tab. Point to the None button in the Setting area of the Borders sheet.**

The Borders and Shading dialog box displays (Figure 1-6).

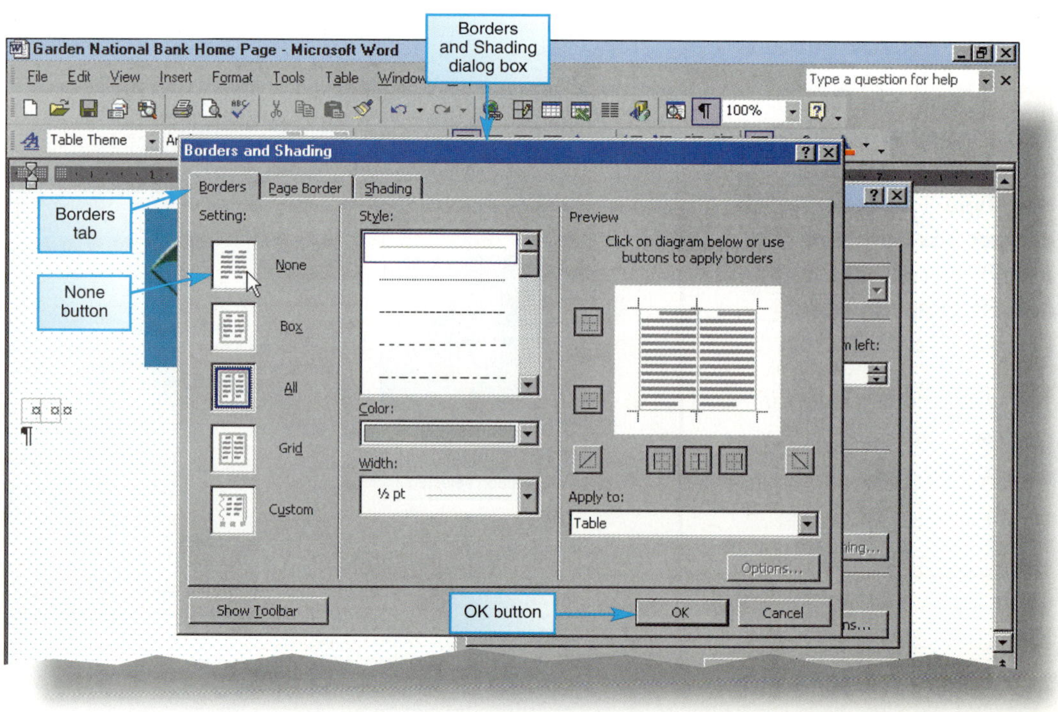

FIGURE 1-6

2 Click the None button in the Setting area and then click the OK button in the Borders and Shading dialog box. Click the OK button in the Table Properties dialog box.

The borderless table displays (Figure 1-7).

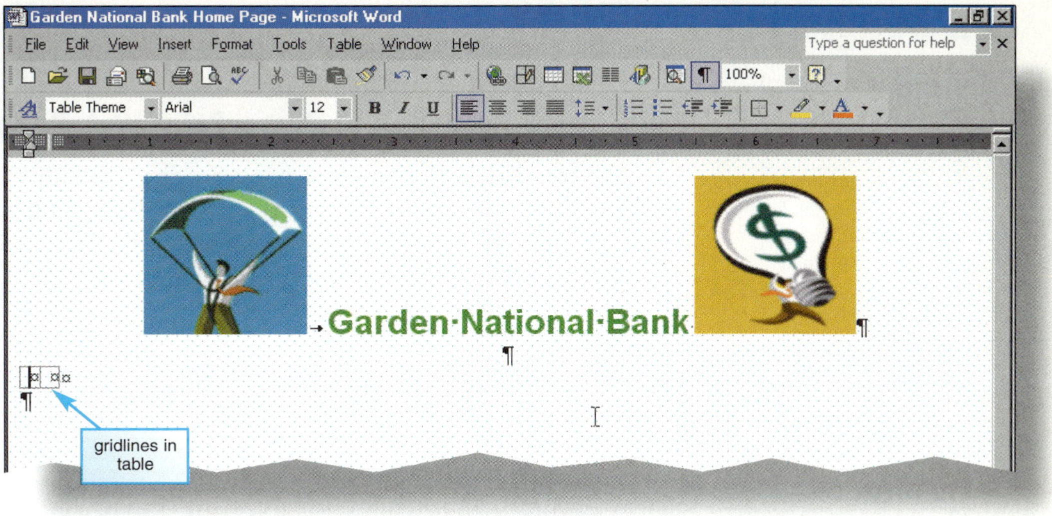

FIGURE 1-7

The border of the table displays with gridlines in the Word document. **Gridlines** can be used as a guide when entering text or images. When the document is viewed in your browser or printed, the table border does not display or print.

Inserting the Text for the Hyperlinks

After creating the borderless table, you must insert the three text phrases that will be used as hyperlinks on the home page. These phrases (About Us, Savings Products, and E-mail Comments) allow you to jump to two other Web pages and create an e-mail message. Perform the steps below to add the text phrases that are used as hyperlinks.

More About

Hyperlinks

In addition to the way in which the hyperlinks are created in this project, you can copy and paste text as a hyperlink. Copy the text you want to the Clipboard, click where you want to insert the text, and then click Paste as Hyperlink on the Edit menu.

Steps To Insert Text for Hyperlinks

1 If necessary, click the leftmost cell in the table.

2 Type `About Us` **and then press the ENTER key twice. Type** `Savings Products` **and then press the ENTER key twice. Type** `E-mail Comments` **as the final text phrase.**

The table displays with the three text phrases that will be used as hyperlinks (Figure 1-8).

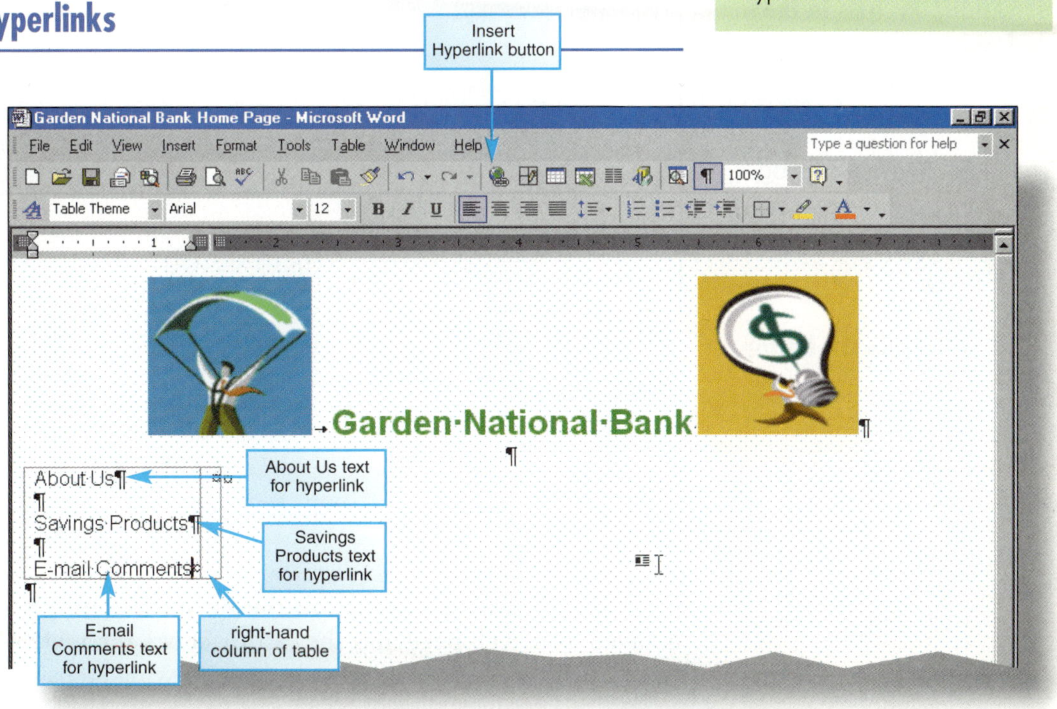

FIGURE 1-8

More About

Hyperlinks

Hyperlinks can link to both external locations and internal locations within the current document. To link to a location inside the current document, select the Place in This Document option in the Link to bar in the Insert Hyperlink dialog box. The Microsoft Office XP application then will provide a list of locations within the current document to which you can link.

With the text phrases added, the next step is to select each text phrase and then insert the corresponding hyperlink.

Inserting a Hyperlink to PowerPoint Web Pages

The **Insert Hyperlink feature** provides the capability of linking to an existing file or Web page, to a place within the current document, to a newly created document, or to an e-mail address. In this project, two text phrases (About Us and Savings Products) will be created that link to Web pages. The About Us hyperlink will jump to a PowerPoint presentation that is saved as a Web page using the Web page name AboutUs.htm. The Savings Products hyperlink will jump to a data access page using the Web page name SavingsProducts.htm. You will create the data access page later from an existing Access database. The third text phrase (E-mail Comments) links to an e-mail address, allowing the Web page visitor to send an e-mail message to the bank manager.

Perform the following steps to create a hyperlink for the first text phrase.

Steps To Create a Hyperlink to PowerPoint Web Pages

1. **Drag through the text, About Us, in the table. Click the Insert Hyperlink button on the Standard toolbar.**

2. **If necessary, click the Existing File or Web Page button on the Link to bar. Type** `a:\AboutUs.htm` **in the Address text box. Point to the OK button.**

   The Insert Hyperlink dialog box displays with the name of the Web page in the Address text box (Figure 1-9).

3. **Click the OK button.**

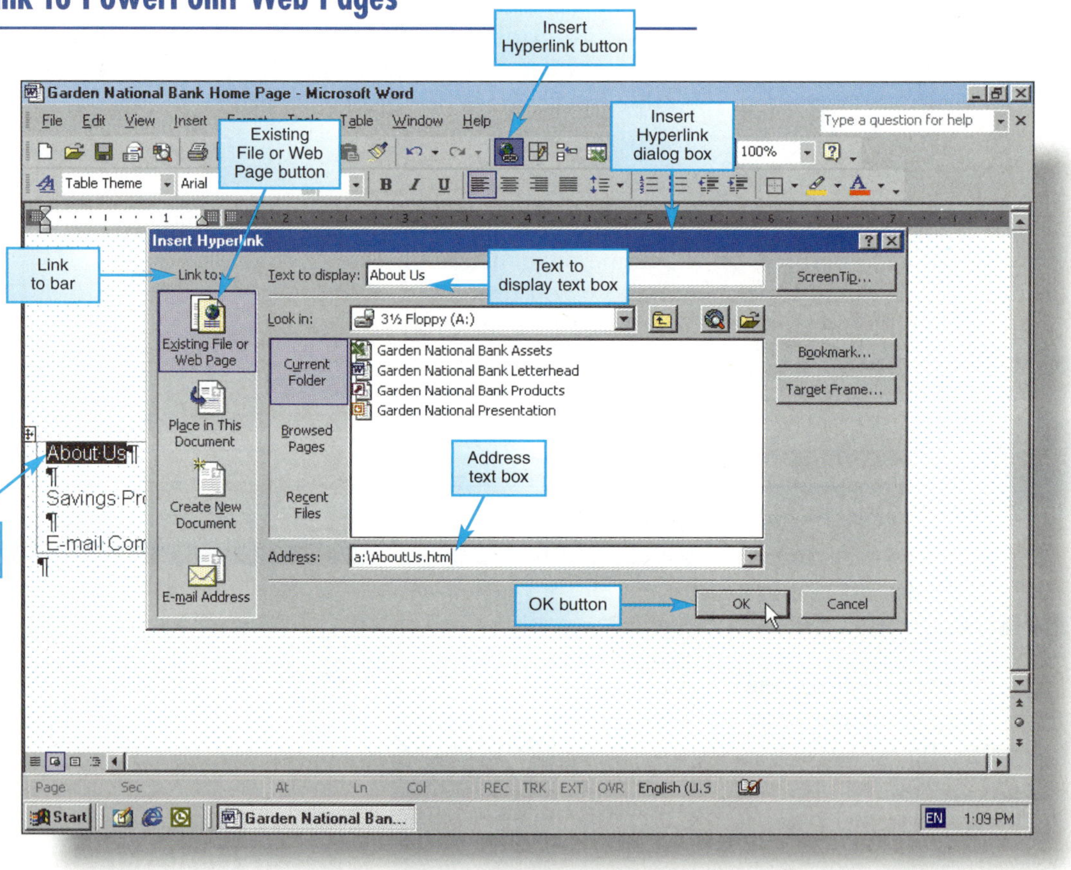

FIGURE 1-9

Other Ways

1. On Insert menu click Hyperlink
2. Right-click selected words, click Hyperlink on shortcut menu
3. Press CTRL+K
4. In Voice Command mode say, "Hyperlink"

The hyperlink is assigned to the About Us text phrase. Once the Word document is saved as a Web page and the visitor clicks the text, About Us, the AboutUs.htm file on drive A displays. Perform the following steps to add the other two hyperlinks.

TO INSERT THE REMAINING HYPERLINKS

1. Drag through the text, Savings Products, in the table. Click the Insert Hyperlink button on the Standard toolbar.
2. Type `a:\SavingsProducts.htm` in the Address text box and then click the OK button.
3. Drag through the text, E-mail Comments. Click the Insert Hyperlink button on the Standard toolbar and then click E-mail Address on the Link to bar.
4. Type `manager@isp.com` in the E-mail address text box and then click the OK button.

The table displays as shown in Figure 1-10.

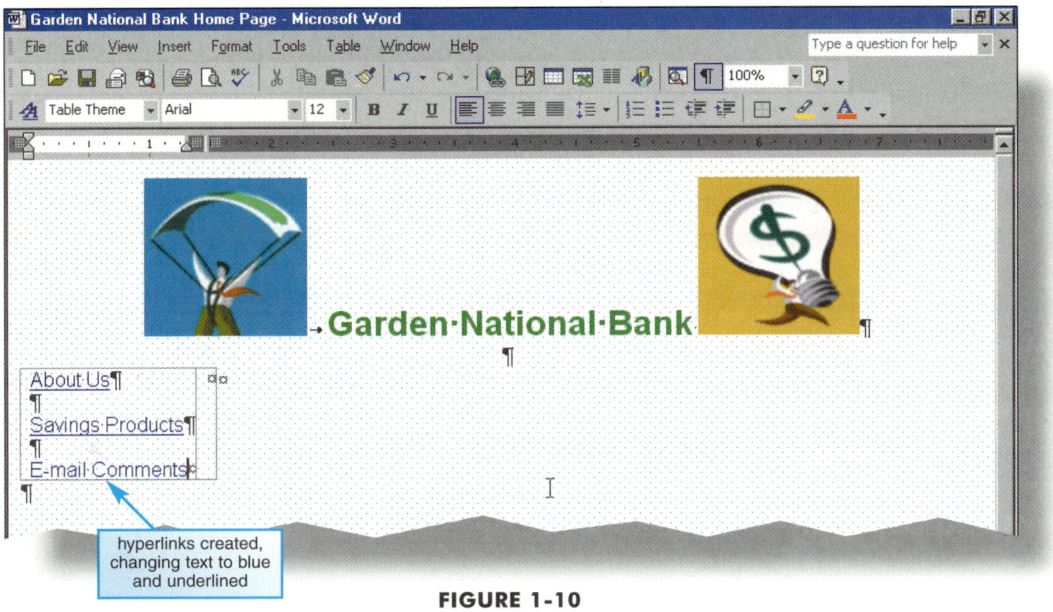

FIGURE 1-10

The three hyperlinks are created. When you click the E-mail Comments hyperlink, it will create an e-mail message to manager@isp.com. The other two hyperlinks (About Us and Savings Products) will not be functional until the corresponding Web pages are created later in this project.

Embedding an Excel Chart into a Word Document

This project uses the **Object Linking and Embedding** (**OLE**) feature of Microsoft Office XP to insert the Excel chart into a Word document. OLE allows you to incorporate parts of a document or entire documents from one application into another.

The Bar chart in Excel is called a **source object** (Figure 1-1b on page I 1.06) and the Garden National Bank Home Page document is the **destination document**. Once an object is embedded, it becomes part of the destination document. This project illustrates using the Paste Special command on the Edit menu to embed the Excel object. The **Paste Special command** inserts an object into Word, but still recognizes the **source program**, the program in which the object was created. When you double-click an embedded object, such as the Bank Assets by Investment Type worksheet, the source program opens and allows you to make changes. In this example, Excel is the source program. With the hyperlinks added to the Word document, the next step is to embed the Bar chart into the Word document. First, open the Excel workbook as shown in the steps on the next page.

More About

Embedded Objects

The advantage of using an integrated set of applications, such as Microsoft Office XP, is the capability of sharing information among applications. The Object Linking and Embedding (OLE) features of Office XP make the integration process more efficient. A chart created in Excel can be included in a Word document using OLE. To edit the embedded object, double-click it. The source program then starts and opens the source object for editing.

TO START EXCEL, CUSTOMIZE EXCEL, AND OPEN AN EXISTING WORKBOOK

1. Click the Start button on the Windows taskbar and then click Open Office Document on the Start menu.
2. Click the Look in box arrow and then click 3½ Floppy (A:) in the Look in list.
3. Double-click the Garden National Bank Assets workbook.
4. If the Language bar displays, click its Minimize button.
5. If the Standard and Formatting toolbars display on one row, click the Toolbar Options button on the right side of either toolbar and then click Show Buttons on Two Rows on the Toolbar Options menu.

The next two sections explain how to embed an Excel chart into a Word document and then resize it. The first section explains embedding a chart into a Word document. Perform the following steps to embed the Excel Bar chart into the Word document.

Steps To Embed an Excel Chart into a Word Document

1. **Click the Bank Assets Chart tab.**

The Bar chart is active and displays (Figure 1-11).

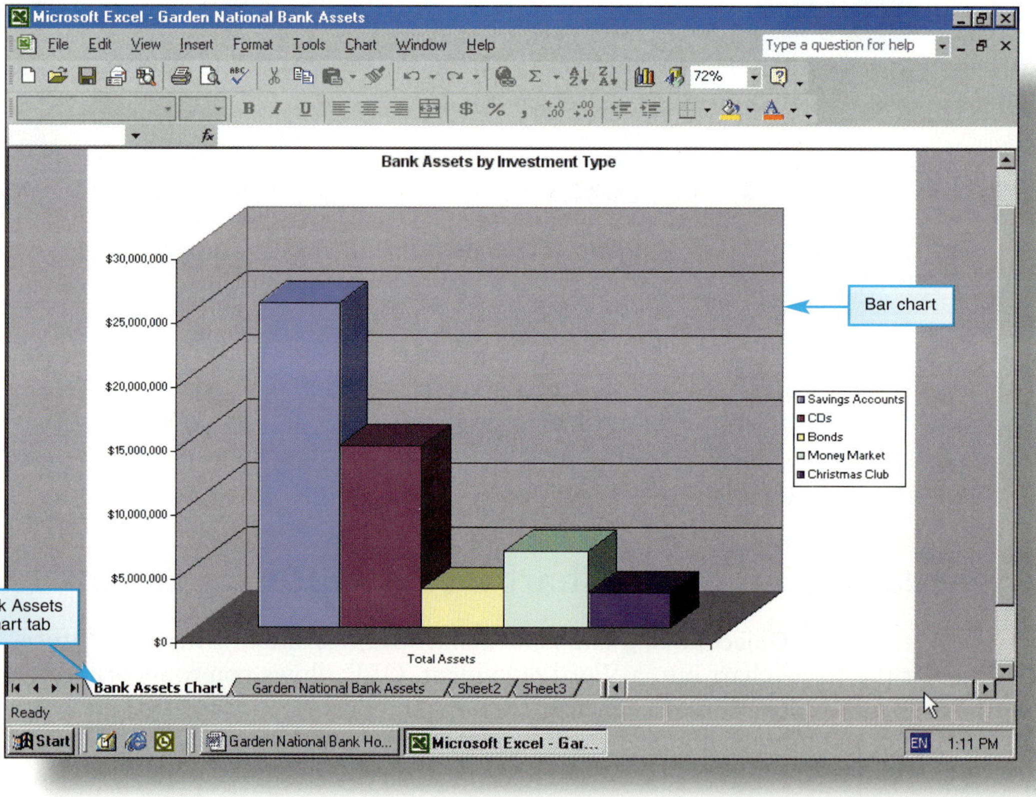

FIGURE 1-11

2 Click the white area around the Chart Area to select the chart and then click the Copy button on the Standard toolbar.

Excel places a copy of the Bar chart on the Office Clipboard. A scrolling marquee displays around the Chart Area (Figure 1-12).

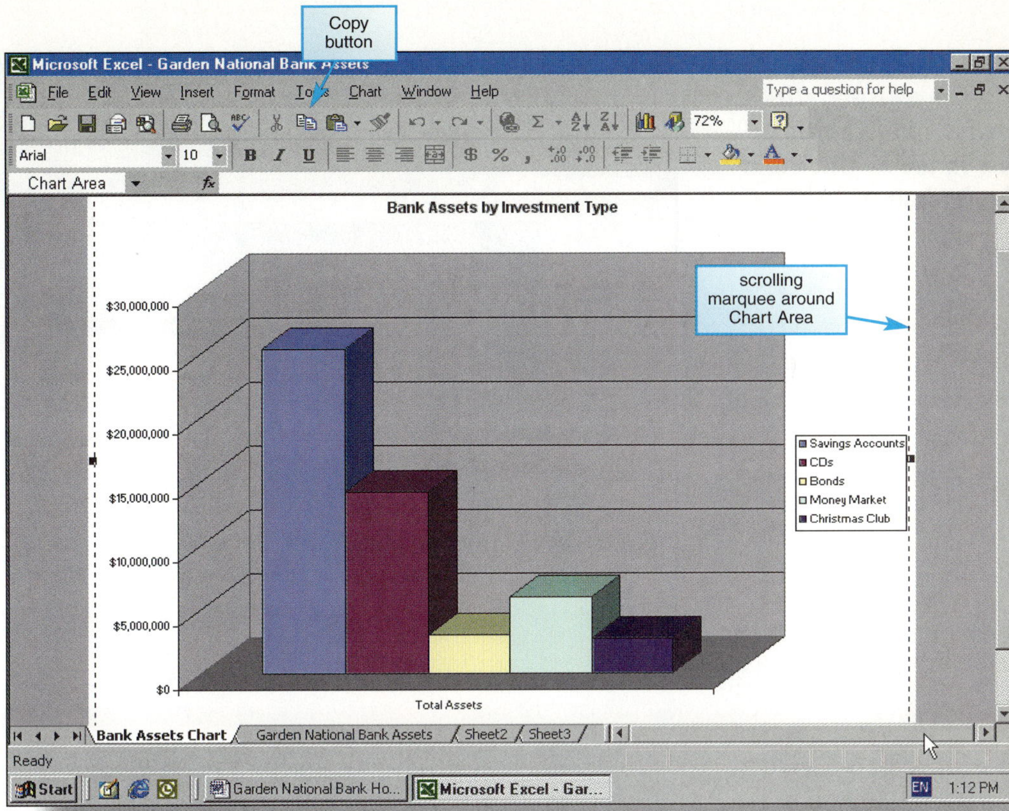

FIGURE 1-12

3 Click the Garden National Bank Home Page button on the taskbar. If necessary, click the right column of the table.

4 Click Edit on the menu bar and then point to Paste Special.

The Edit menu displays and the Paste Special command is highlighted (Figure 1-13).

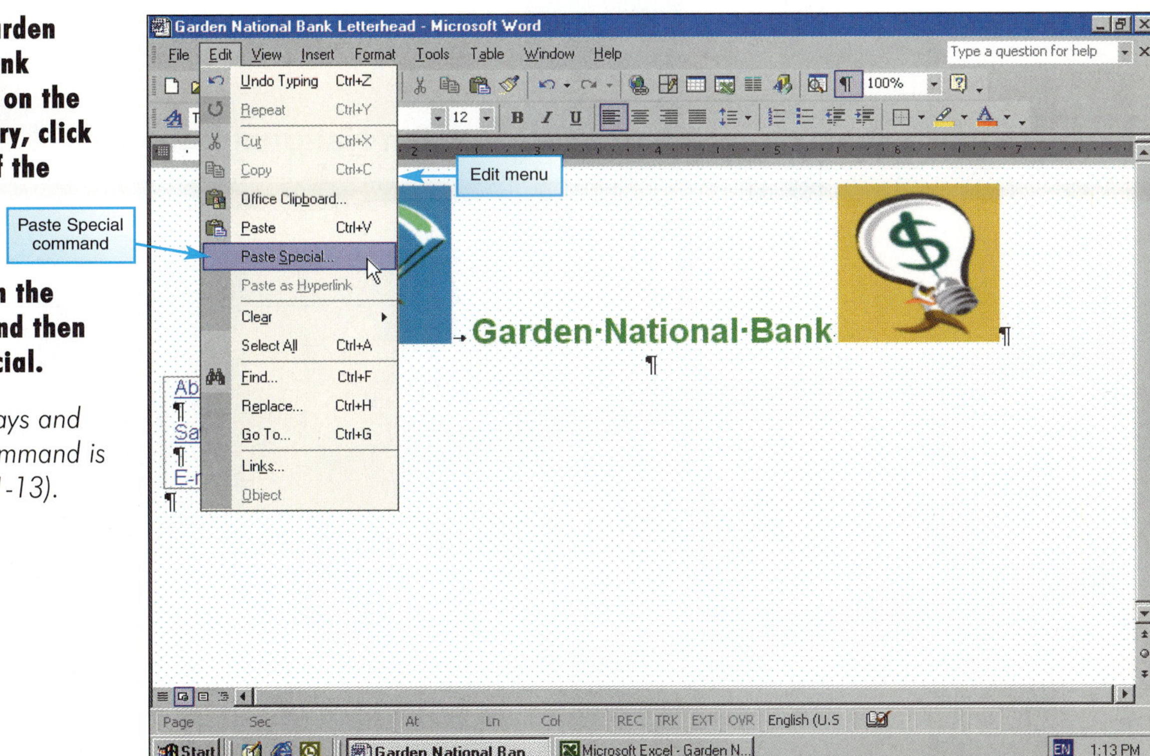

FIGURE 1-13

5 Click Paste Special. If necessary, click Microsoft Excel Chart Object in the As list. Point to the OK button.

The Paste Special dialog box displays (Figure 1-14). The Paste option button is selected. Microsoft Excel Chart Object displays in the As list.

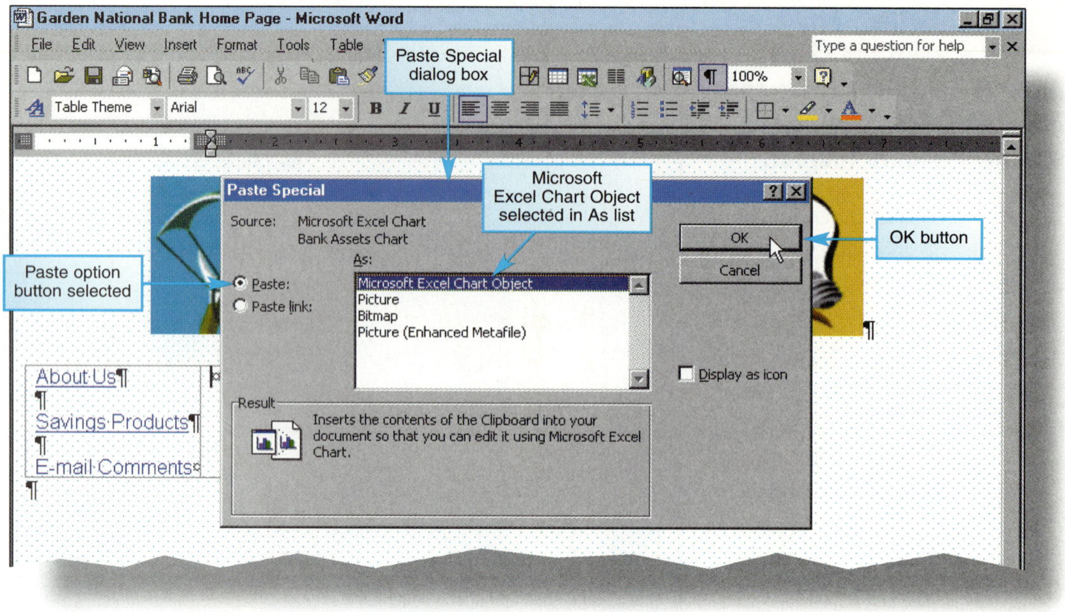

FIGURE 1-14

6 Click the OK button.

Word embeds the Bar chart into the document (Figure 1-15).

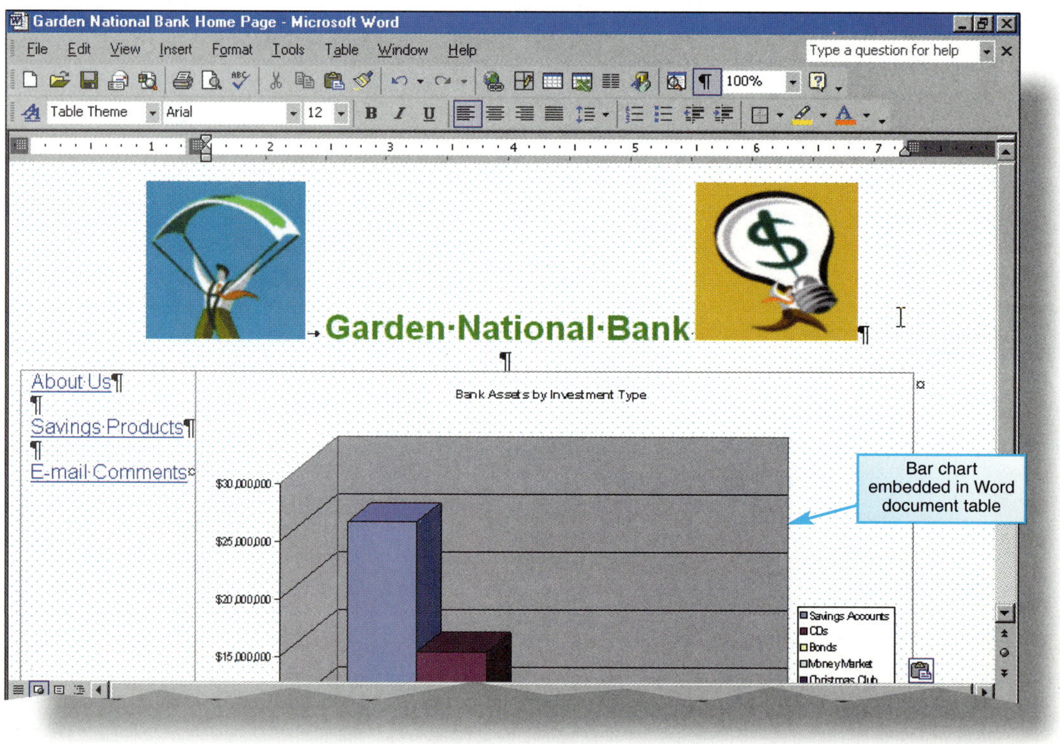

FIGURE 1-15

Other Ways

1. On Edit Menu click Copy
2. Press CTRL+C
3. In Voice Command mode say, "Copy"

Changing the Size of an Embedded Object

The embedded Bar chart exceeds the margins of the Garden National Bank Home Page document. Reducing the size of the Bar chart will improve the layout of the document. In this project, you will use the Format Object dialog box to change the size of the chart.

All Microsoft Office XP applications allow you to use three methods to copy objects between applications: (1) copy and paste; (2) copy and embed; and (3) copy and link. The first method uses the Copy and Paste buttons. The latter two use the Paste Special command. Table 1-1 summarizes the differences among the three methods.

More About

Objects

Objects can be nearly any part of an Office XP application or other Windows application. Some examples are Excel worksheets, a paragraph in a Word document, and a slide in a PowerPoint presentation. As long as you use the Paste Special command to paste data on the Clipboard, you can keep data in its native format.

Table 1-1 Copy Methods

METHOD	*CHARACTERISTICS*
Copy and paste	The source document becomes part of the destination document. An object may be edited, but the editing features are limited to those of the destination application. An Excel worksheet becomes a Word table. If changes are made to values in the Word table, any original Excel formulas are not recalculated.
Copy and embed	The source document becomes part of the destination document. An object may be edited in the destination document using source editing features. The Excel worksheet remains a worksheet in Word. If you make changes to values in the worksheet with Word active, Excel formulas will be recalculated. If, however, you change the worksheet in Excel without the document open in Word, these changes will not display in the Word document the next time you open it.
Copy and link	The source document does not become part of the destination document, even though it appears to be. Instead, a link is established between the two documents, so that when you open the Word document, the worksheet displays within the document, as though it were a part of it. When you attempt to edit a linked worksheet in Word, the system activates Excel. If you change the worksheet in Excel, the changes also will display in the Word document the next time you open it.

Perform the following steps to reduce the size of the chart using the Object command on the Format menu.

Steps To Change the Size of an Embedded Object

1 If necessary, click the Bar chart to select it. Click Format on the menu bar and then point to Object.

The Bar chart is selected as indicated by sizing handles on the selection rectangle. The Format menu displays, and the Object command is highlighted (Figure 1-16).

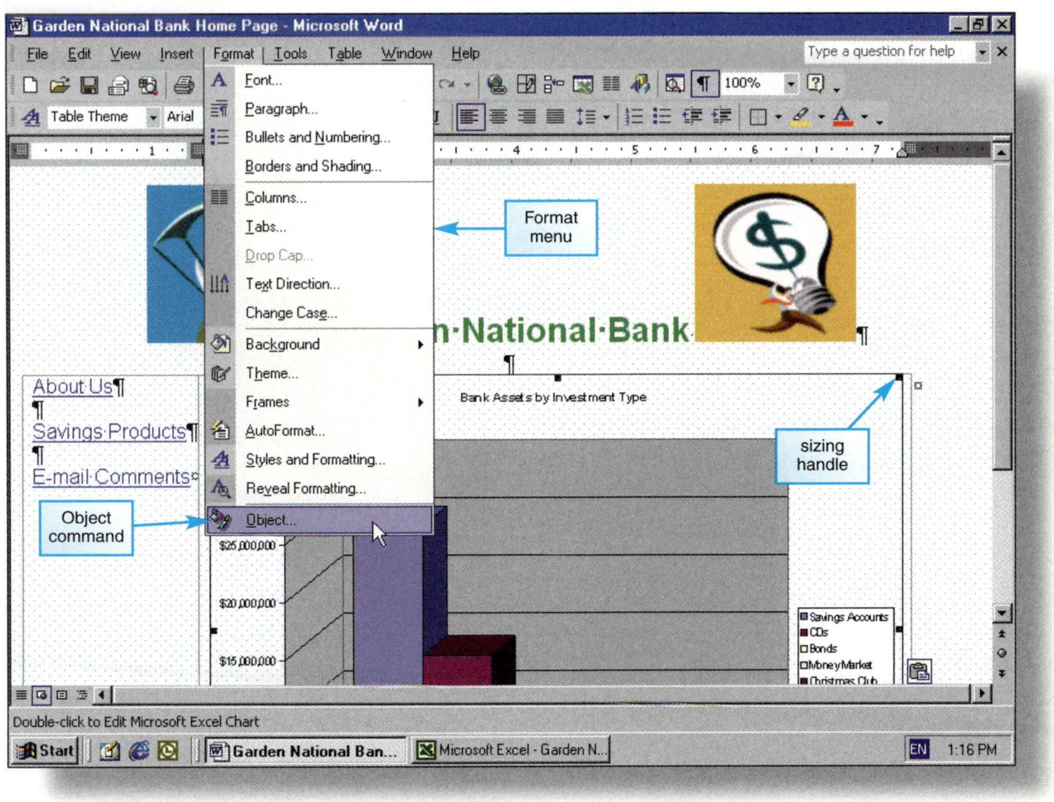

FIGURE 1-16

2 Click Object. If necessary, click the Size tab.

The Format Object dialog box and Size sheet display (Figure 1-17).

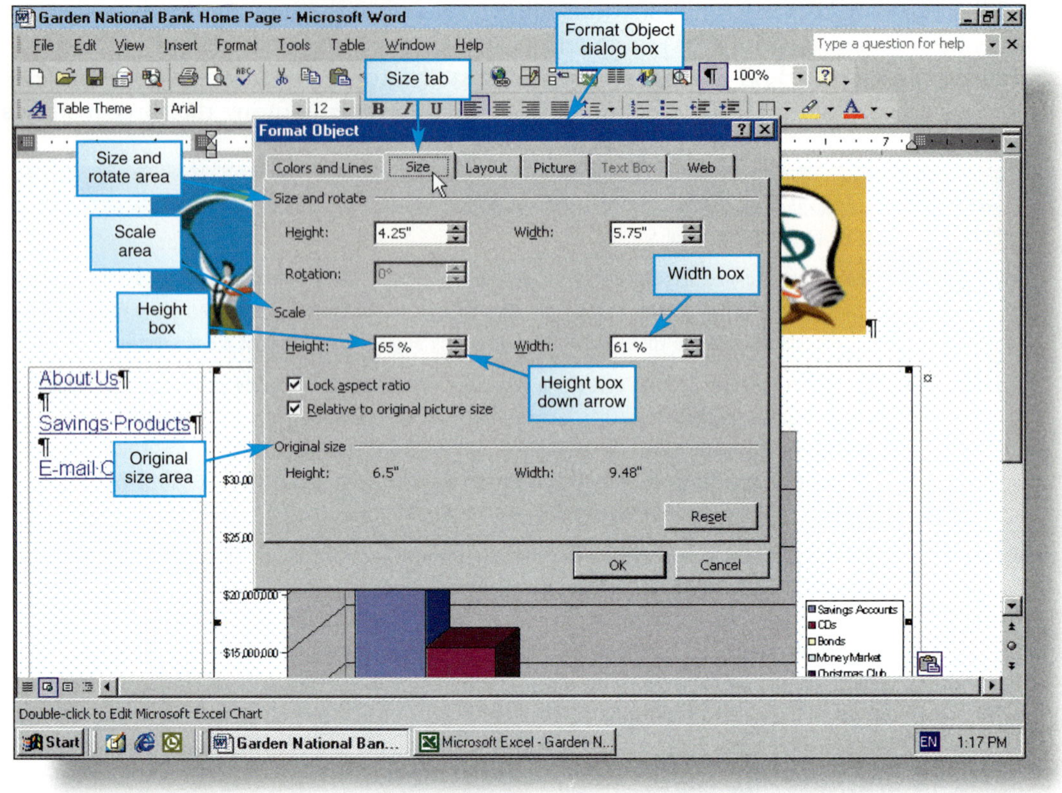

FIGURE 1-17

3 In the Scale area, if necessary, click the Height box up or down arrow or the Width box up or down arrow until 65 % displays in both the Height box and the Width box. Point to the OK button.

The Height box and the Width box both display 65 % (Figure 1-18). Depending on the size of the object when it was pasted into the Word document, you may need to scale either up or down in the Scale area Height and Width boxes. When you change the value in either the Height or Width box, both values change because the Lock aspect ratio check box is selected.

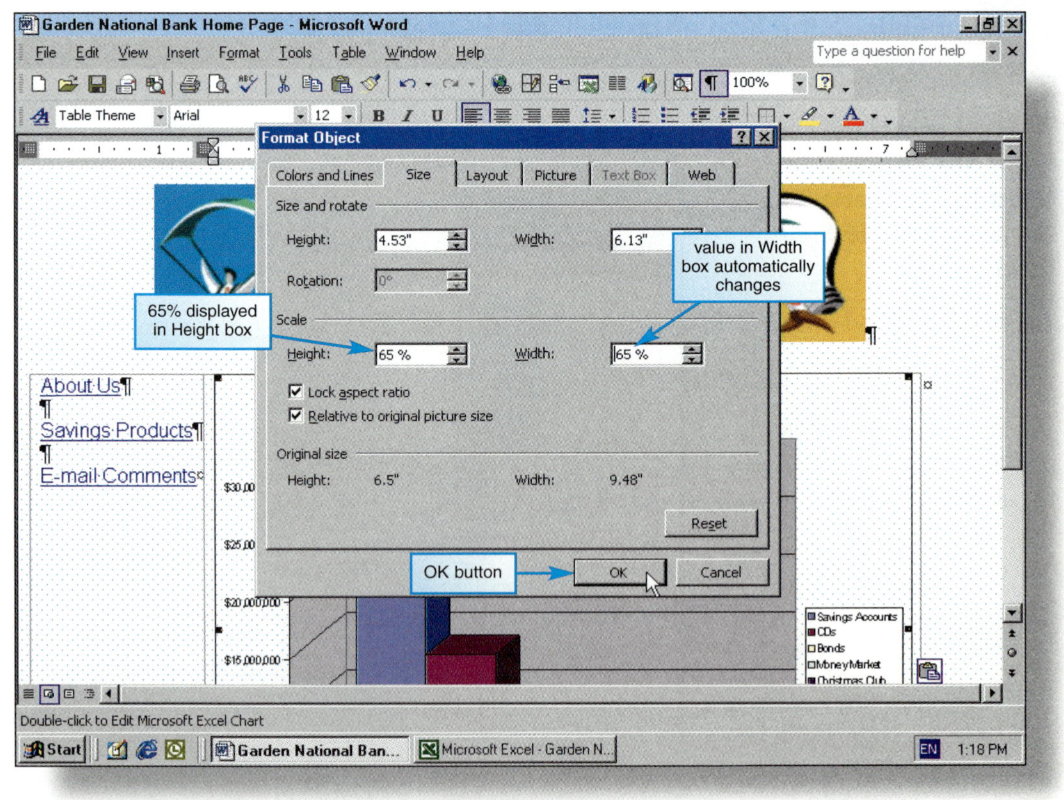

FIGURE 1-18

4 Click the OK button. If necessary, scroll to see the embedded chart.

Word reduces the size of the chart to 65% of its original size (Figure 1-19).

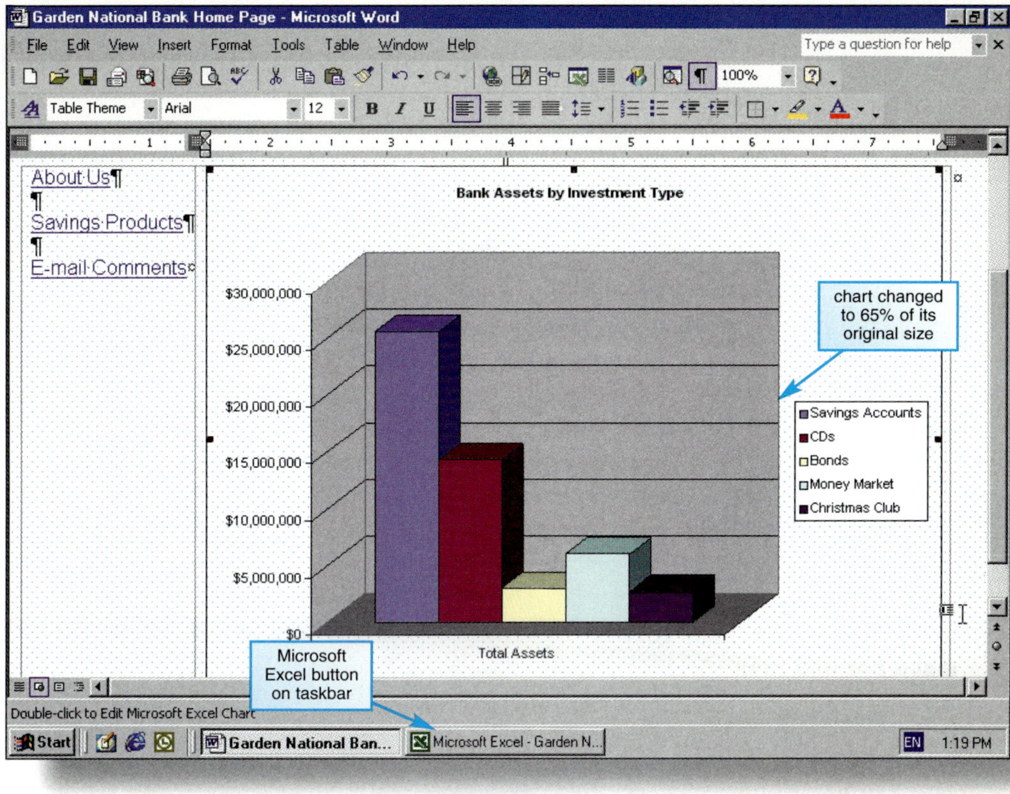

FIGURE 1-19

Other Ways

1. Right-click Bar chart, click Format Object on shortcut menu
2. Select Bar chart, then in Voice Command mode say, "Format Object"

The Format Object dialog box contains two areas that can change the size of an object. The **Size and rotate area** allows you to increase or decrease the height or width of an object in inches. When available, it also allows you to rotate the object in degrees around an axis. The **Scale area** allows you to change the size of an object by a specific percentage while maintaining the height-to-width ratio. The height-to-width ratio is referred to as **aspect ratio**. You change the height and width independently by deselecting the Lock aspect ratio check box. The **Original size area** at the bottom of the Format Object dialog box displays the original height and width of the selected object.

More About

Resizing

To resize an image proportionally from a corner, you can press and hold down the SHIFT key while dragging a corner sizing handle. To resize vertically, horizontally, or diagonally from the center outward, press and hold down the CTRL key while dragging a sizing handle. To resize proportionally from the center outward, press and hold down the CTRL+SHIFT keys and drag a corner sizing handle.

Quitting Excel

With the Bar chart embedded in the Word document, you no longer need the Garden National Bank Sales workbook open. Perform the following steps to quit Excel.

TO QUIT EXCEL

1. Right-click the Microsoft Excel - Garden National Bank Assests button on the taskbar. Click Close on the shortcut menu. If prompted to save changes, click the No button.
2. If the Microsoft Excel dialog box displays regarding saving the large amount of information on the Clipboard, click the No button.

Adding Scrolling Text to a Word Document

The Word document is almost ready to be saved as a Web page. The final item that needs to be added is something that will capture the attention of your Web page visitor. One of the attention-grabbing techniques that Web developers use is scrolling marquees. A **scrolling marquee** is a line of text that moves across the Web page. Generally, scrolling text is used to highlight information about the Web site. With Word 2002, you can create scrolling text using the **Scrolling Text button** on the Web Tools toolbar. A scrolling marquee will be created just below the Garden National Bank heading.

In order to create scrolling text, the Web Tools toolbar must display. Perform the following steps to display the Web Tools toolbar.

Steps To Display the Web Tools Toolbar

1 Click View on the menu bar and then point to Toolbars. Point to Web Tools on the Toolbars submenu.

2 Click Web Tools. If necessary, point to the Web Tools toolbar title bar and drag the toolbar to the center, right side of the window.

The Web Tools toolbar displays (Figure 1-20).

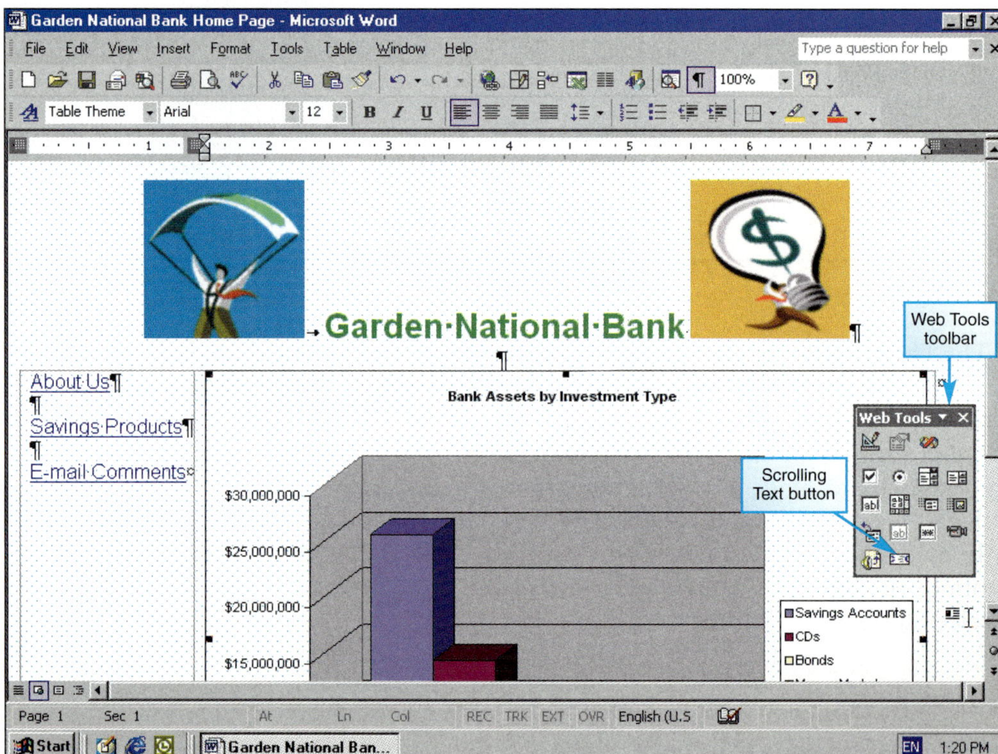

FIGURE 1-20

The **Web Tools toolbar** is used to create the scrolling text that moves under the Web page heading.

Inserting Scrolling Text

A number of options are available for scrolling text. The **behavior** of the text specifies the manner in which the text moves on the Web page. By default, the behavior of the line of text is to scroll. **Scrolling** moves the text in from one side and off the other side of the Web page. Another behavior option is to slide the text. Setting the behavior to **slide** moves the text in from one side of the Web page and stops as soon as the text touches the opposite side. The third option is to set text behavior to alternate. **Alternate** bounces the text back and forth in the margins of the marquee. The default behavior is scrolling text. In this project, the scrolling text behavior is changed to slide, as shown in the following steps.

Steps To Insert Scrolling Text into a Word Document

1 Click the paragraph mark below the Garden National Bank heading and then click the Scrolling Text button on the Web Tools toolbar.

The Scrolling Text dialog box displays (Figure 1-21).

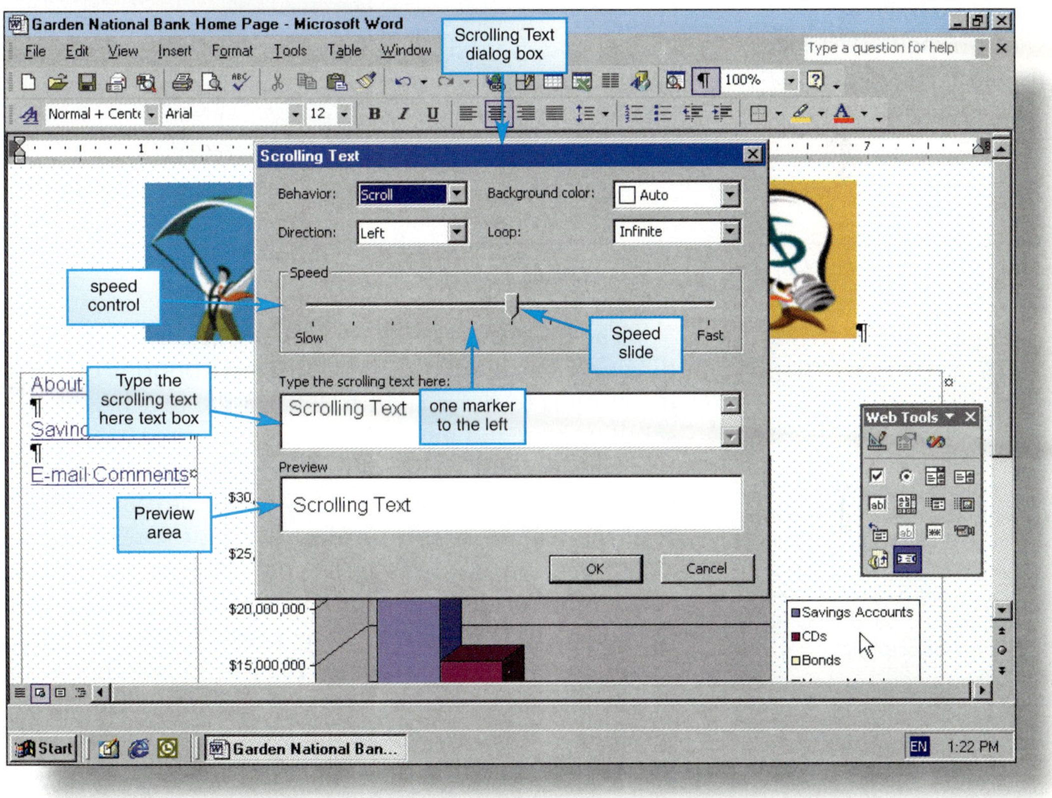

FIGURE 1-21

2 **Click the Behavior box arrow and then click Slide in the list.**

3 **Drag through the text, Scrolling Text, in the Type the scrolling text here text box. Type** `2533 Main Street, Anton, IL 60323 (630) 555-3939` **as the scrolling text.**

4 **Drag the Speed slide one speed marker to the left and then click the OK button.**

The scrolling text displays (Figure 1-22).

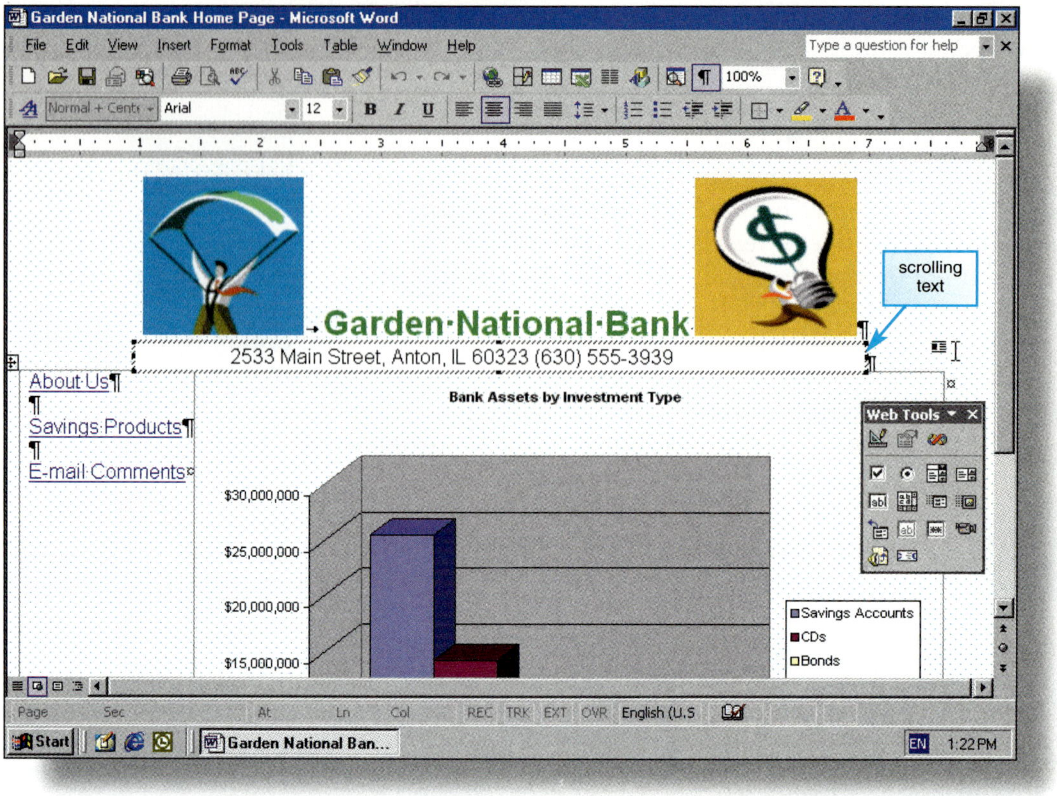

FIGURE 1-22

More About

Scrolling Text

To format the text, use the Font command on the Format menu while you are in Design mode. You turn off Design mode to see the results. In browsers that do not support scrolling text, the text will display but it will not be scrolling.

The **direction** of the text movement can be left to right or right to left. The direction attribute in the scrolling text options controls this movement. The default direction is to move right to left, so the text begins in the right margin of the line of scrolling text and moves to the left.

The **speed** of the scrolling text also can be varied from slow to fast. Scrolling the text too fast cancels the benefits of the scrolling text. If the Web page visitor cannot read the text because it scrolls too fast, the text serves no purpose.

Other options that can be controlled in scrolling text are background colors and the number of times to loop the scrolling text. The **background** attribute determines the color of the line of scrolling text. The background default is a transparent background, so the background of the line of scrolling text displays the background color of whatever is behind it. The **loop** attribute determines the number of times that the scrolling text moves across the Web page. The default is an infinite loop, which means the text will scroll indefinitely, but the loop can be set to a specific number of times.

The default direction, background color, and loop are used for the scrolling text that is inserted into the Word document. Slide was selected as the behavior for the scrolling text. Because of that, the text scrolls from the right margin and stops scrolling when it reaches the left margin. The next section explains how to resize the scrolling text.

Resizing the Scrolling Text

The default for scrolling text is to move the text all the way across the Web page from the right margin of the page to the left margin. Sometimes, it is better to shorten the distance of the scrolling text. In this project, the scrolling text is centered below the Garden National Bank heading of the Word document. The Web page visitor sees the company name with address and telephone number information below it. The Design Mode is used in this project to change the size of the scrolling text. In general, **Design Mode** allows you to rearrange and design the page in a user-friendly manner.

Perform the following steps to change the size of the scrolling text.

Steps To Resize the Scrolling Text

1 Click the Design Mode button on the Web Tools toolbar.

2 If necessary, click anywhere within the scrolling text box to select the text. Point to the center sizing handle on the right side of the text box.

The text box displays as shown in Figure 1-23.

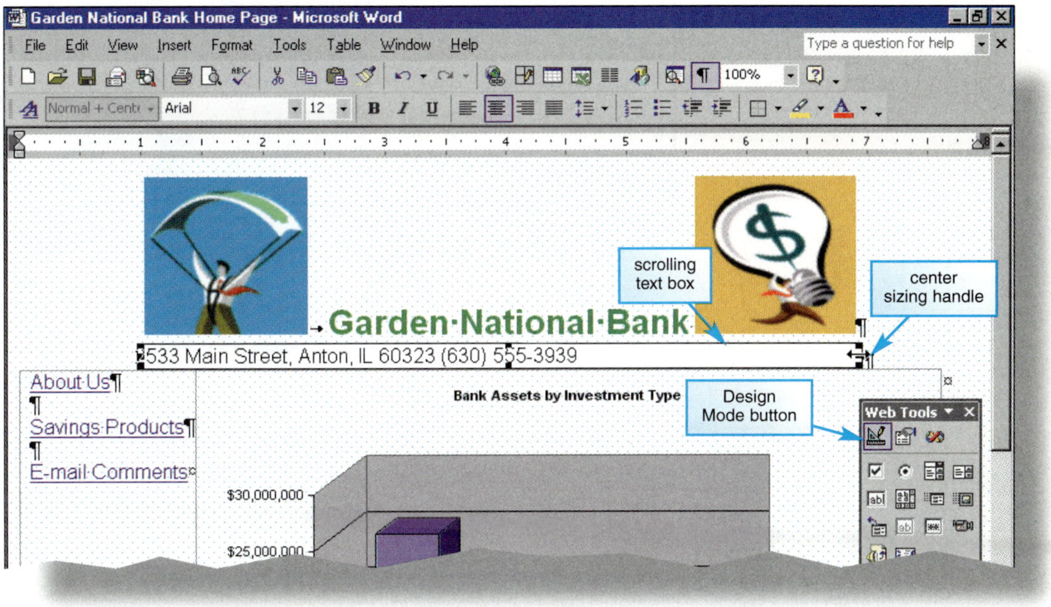

FIGURE 1-23

3 Drag the center sizing handle to the left, so that it is positioned approximately as shown in Figure 1-24.

The dotted line shows the proposed size for the scrolling text.

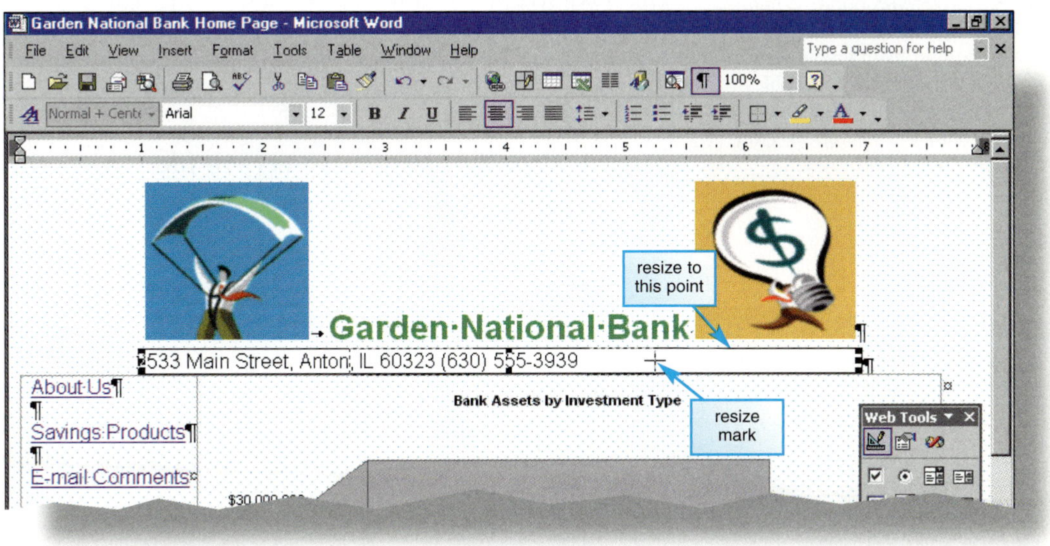

FIGURE 1-24

4 Release the mouse button.

The scrolling text box is resized (Figure 1-25).

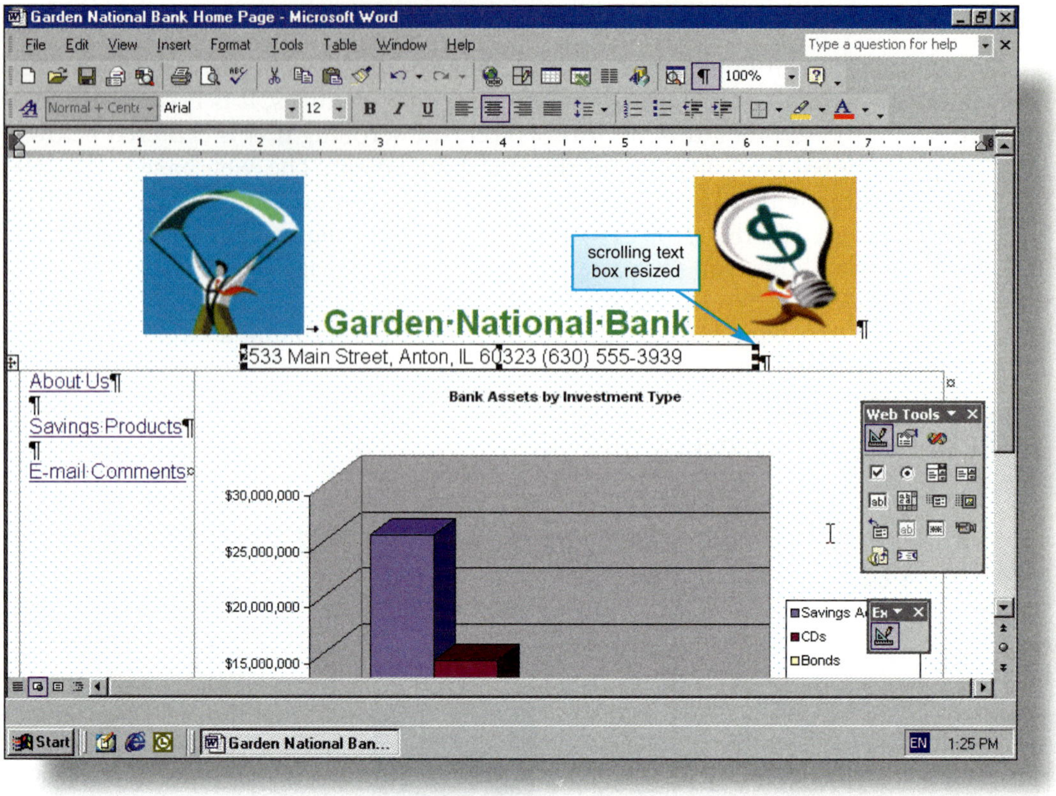

FIGURE 1-25

More About

Web Page Formatting

Because Word provides formatting options that most Web browsers do not support, some text and graphics may look different when you view them on a Web page. When creating documents for the Web, using Web layout view will ensure that your graphics look the way you want them to when they are viewed as Web pages in a Web browser.

The home page for the Garden National Bank Web site is complete. The Web page should be viewed in your browser to verify that it is correct.

Viewing the Word Document in Your Browser and Saving It as a Web Page

The next step is to view the Word document in your browser to verify that all information is accurate. After verifying its accuracy, you then can save the Word document as an HTML file. Saving the Word document as an HTML file makes it possible for it to be viewed using a browser, such as Internet Explorer.

Perform the following steps to preview the document in your browser and then save the Word document as an HTML file.

Steps To Preview the Web Page

1 Click File on the menu bar and then point to Web Page Preview.

2 Click Web Page Preview. If necessary, click the Maximize button on your browser's title bar.

The Web page displays (Figure 1-26).

3 Click the browser's Close button.

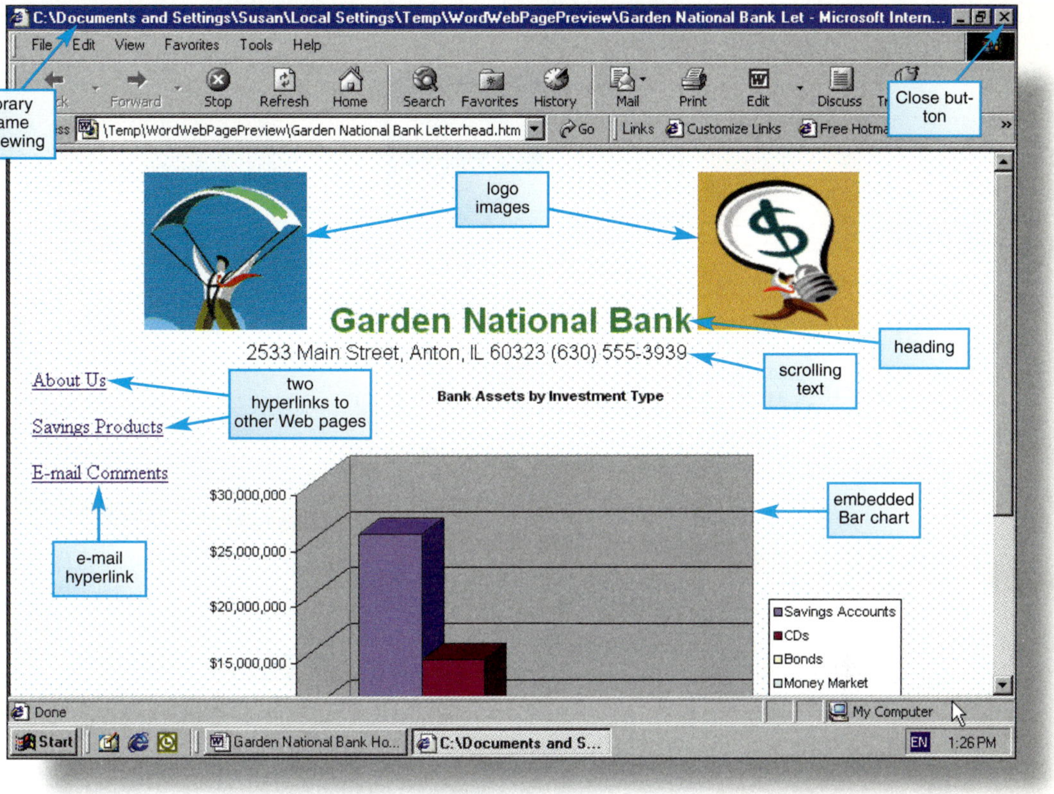

FIGURE 1-26

Other Ways

1. Press ALT+F, type B
2. In Voice Command mode say, "File, Web Page Preview"

Verify that the Web page contains all information necessary and displays as shown in Figure 1-26. The Web page consists of a heading with an image and the company name. Below that is a single line of scrolling text that scrolls in from the right margin and stops when it reaches the left margin. Next is a borderless table with three hyperlinks in the left column and a Bar chart in the right column. The E-mail Comments hyperlink should work appropriately when you click it, displaying a new message. The other two links, About Us and Savings Products, do not work because the corresponding Web pages are not available until later in this project.

If the Web page is correct, save it on the Integration Data Disk as an HTML file. If changes need to be made to the Web page, return to the Word document and correct it. Perform the following steps to save the document as a Web page.

TO SAVE A DOCUMENT WITH A NEW FILE NAME

1. Click File on the menu bar and then click Save As Web page.
2. Type `GNBHome` in the File name text box.
3. If necessary, click the Save in box arrow and then click 3½ Floppy (A:) in the Save in list.
4. Click the Save button in the Save As dialog box.

The GNBHome Web page displays in the Word window (Figure 1-27 on the next page).

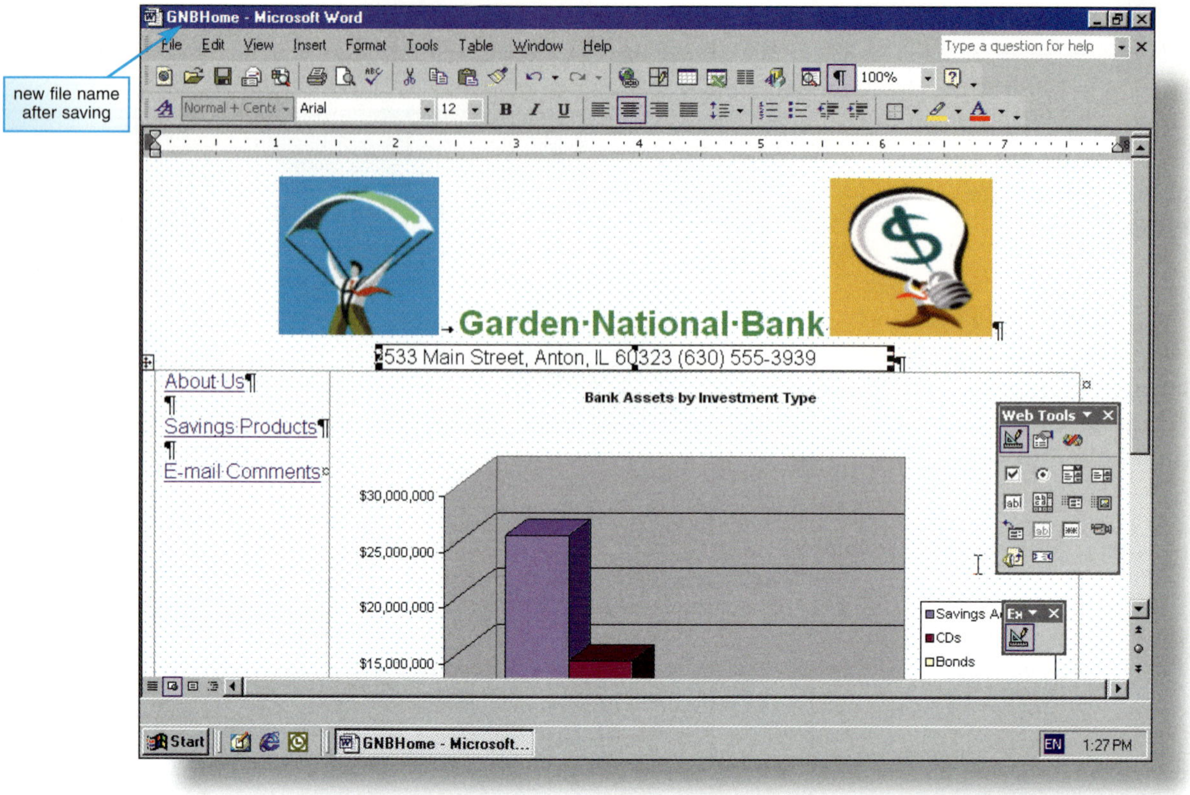

FIGURE 1-27

> **More About**
>
> **Web Programming Languages**
>
> A number of programming languages can be used to create Web pages. Web pages created using the Save as Web Page command on the File menu can be enhanced with other Web programming languages, such as ASP, DHTML, and JavaScript.

Saving an existing Word document as a Web page allows you quickly to get a Word document ready for copying to the Web or to an intranet. One alternative to this is to directly write the hypertext markup language (HTML) to develop the Web pages. **HTML** is a programming language used for Web page creation. The home page created earlier in this project could be created by writing HTML tags (code). For documents that already are in Word format, the easier method is to use the Word's Save as Web Page command. This essentially creates the HTML code for you and saves it in a file. Perform the following step to quit Word.

TO QUIT WORD

1. Click the Close button on the Microsoft Word title bar.

The next step in creating the Web site for Garden National Bank is to save a PowerPoint presentation as an HTML file. The following sections describe how to open a PowerPoint presentation, add a hyperlink to the first page, and save the presentation as an HTML file.

Creating a PowerPoint Presentation Web Page

PowerPoint is a powerful software tool often used to assist in the presentation of information to groups of people. **PowerPoint 2002** allows you to create Web pages from an existing PowerPoint presentation, using the Save as Web Page command. The presentation then can be viewed using your browser.

The PowerPoint presentation used in this project consists of three slides (Figure 1-1g on page I 1.07). The first page is a title slide, containing the bank name and graphics. The second slide contains information about the Garden National Bank staff, with names and job responsibilities. The last slide contains information about the Garden National Bank's savings product lines. This information can be used in its present format to enhance a presentation about the bank. As Web pages, you can use this presentation to address a much wider, global audience on the World Wide Web.

Perform the following steps to open an existing PowerPoint presentation.

TO START POWERPOINT, CUSTOMIZE POWERPOINT, AND OPEN AN EXISTING PRESENTATION

1. Click the Start button on the Windows taskbar and then click Open Office Document on the Start menu.
2. Click the Look in box arrow and then click 3½ Floppy (A:) in the Look in list.
3. Double-click the Garden National Presentation name.
4. If the Language bar displays, click its Minimize button.
5. If the Standard and Formatting toolbars display on one row, click the Toolbar Options button on the right side of either toolbar and then click Show Buttons on Two Rows on the Toolbar Options menu.

The first slide of the PowerPoint presentation displays (Figure 1-28).

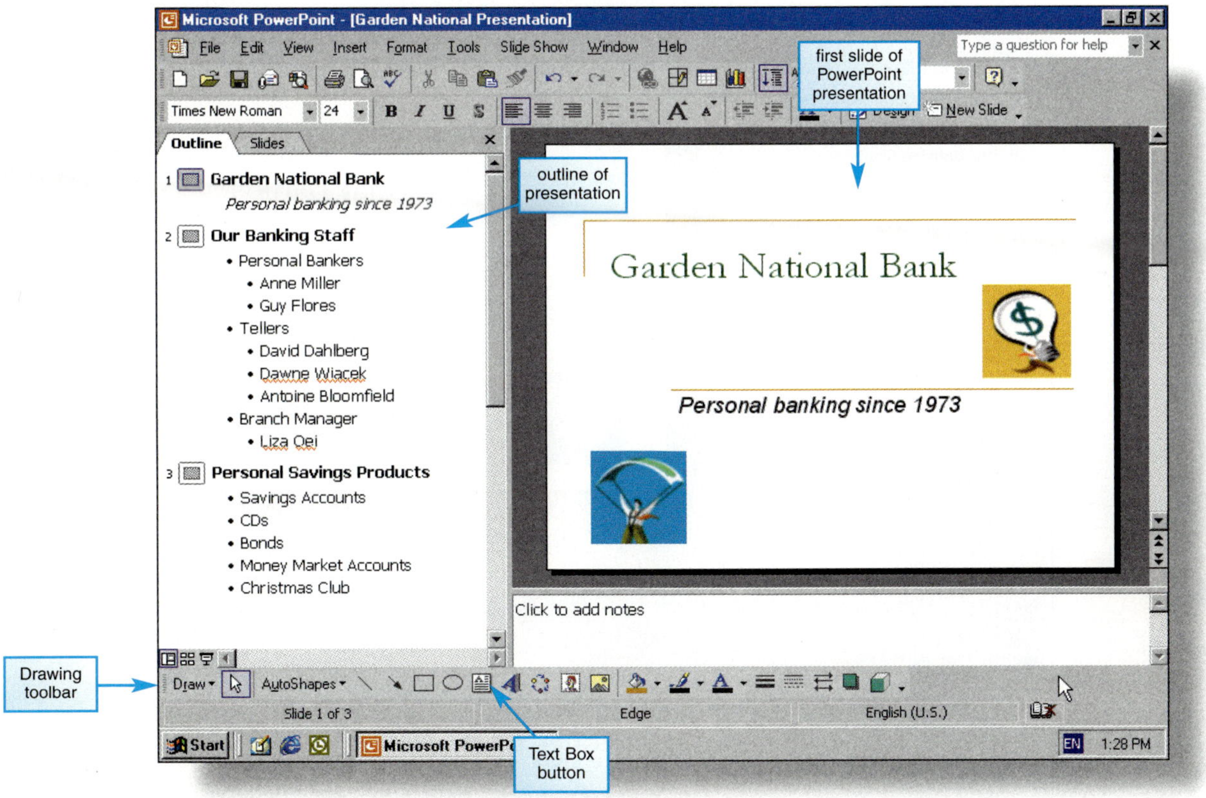

FIGURE 1-28

The PowerPoint presentation now is open. The next step is to add a hyperlink on the first page of the presentation that allows the Web page visitor to return to the Garden National Bank home page.

Adding Text for a Hyperlink

More About

Keeping Links Fresh

When you create a Web page, it is important to make sure that all of your hyperlinks are functional as time goes on. Links to other pages can become stale, or non-functional, if another Web page creator or an external site takes a page offline. Automated tools can help you identify when pages to which you are hyperlinking no longer are available.

One of the more important features of Web sites is their capability of linking from one Web page to another using hyperlinks. In earlier steps in this project, you added three hyperlinks to the Garden National Bank home page. Once Web page visitors link to the PowerPoint Web pages, however, they cannot return to the home page without using the Back button on the browser's toolbar. This is not a convenient way for Web page visitors to navigate through the Web site. In this section, you will add a Home link to the first slide of the PowerPoint presentation (Figure 1-1e on page I 1.07).

Perform the following steps to add the text that will be used as a hyperlink on the PowerPoint Web page.

TO ADD TEXT FOR A HYPERLINK INTO A POWERPOINT PRESENTATION

1. Click the Text Box button on the Drawing toolbar.
2. Click in the lower-right corner of the first page of the PowerPoint presentation.
3. Type `Home` as the hyperlink text.

The text box displays (Figure 1-29).

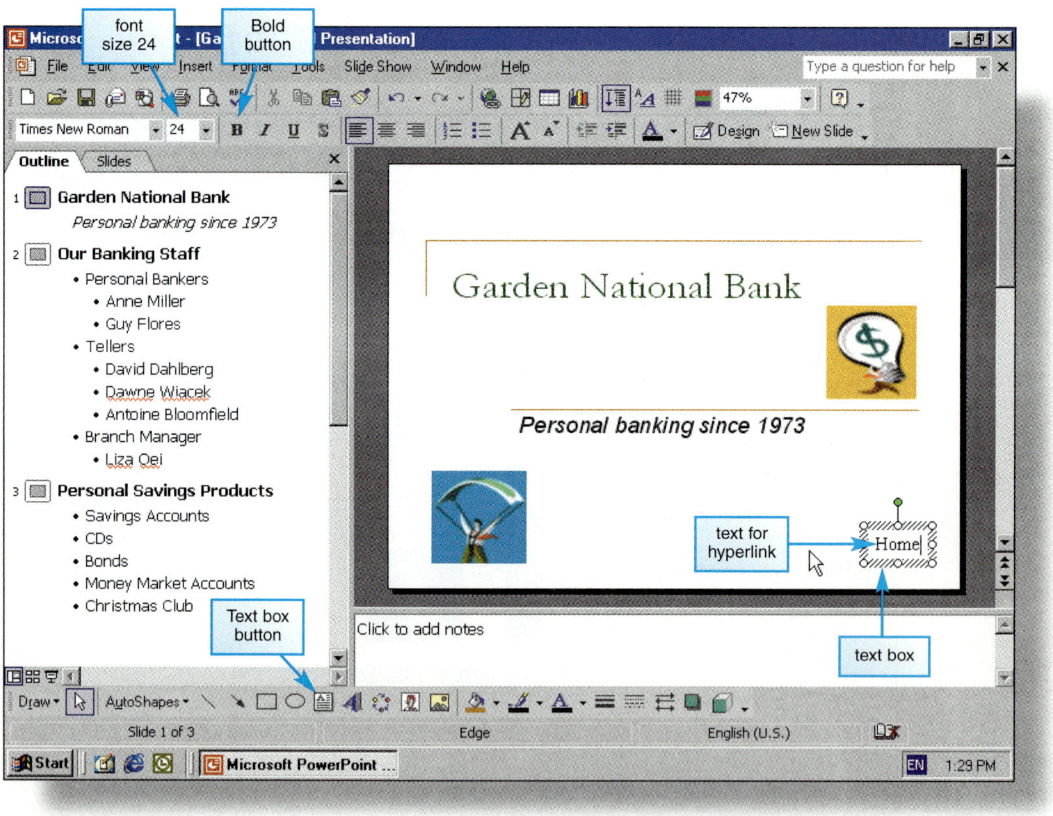

FIGURE 1-29

Other Ways

1. On Insert menu click Text Box
2. Press ALT+I, type X
3. In Voice Command mode say, "Insert, Text Box"

Creating a Hyperlink

After you enter the text for the hyperlink, you can create the hyperlink itself. When clicked, the hyperlink jumps to the Garden National Bank home page created previously in this project and saved on drive A. To create the hyperlink, you will use the Insert Hyperlink button on the Standard toolbar.

Perform the following steps to create the PowerPoint hyperlink.

Steps To Insert a Hyperlink into a PowerPoint Presentation

1 Double-click the word, Home, inside the text box you just inserted.

2 If necessary, click the Font Size box arrow and then click 24. Click the Bold button on the Formatting toolbar.

3 Click the Insert Hyperlink button on the Standard toolbar.

4 If necessary, click the Existing File or Web Page button on the Link to bar. Type `a:\GNBHome.htm` **in the Address text box. Click the OK button.**

Slide 1 of the presentation displays as shown in Figure 1-30.

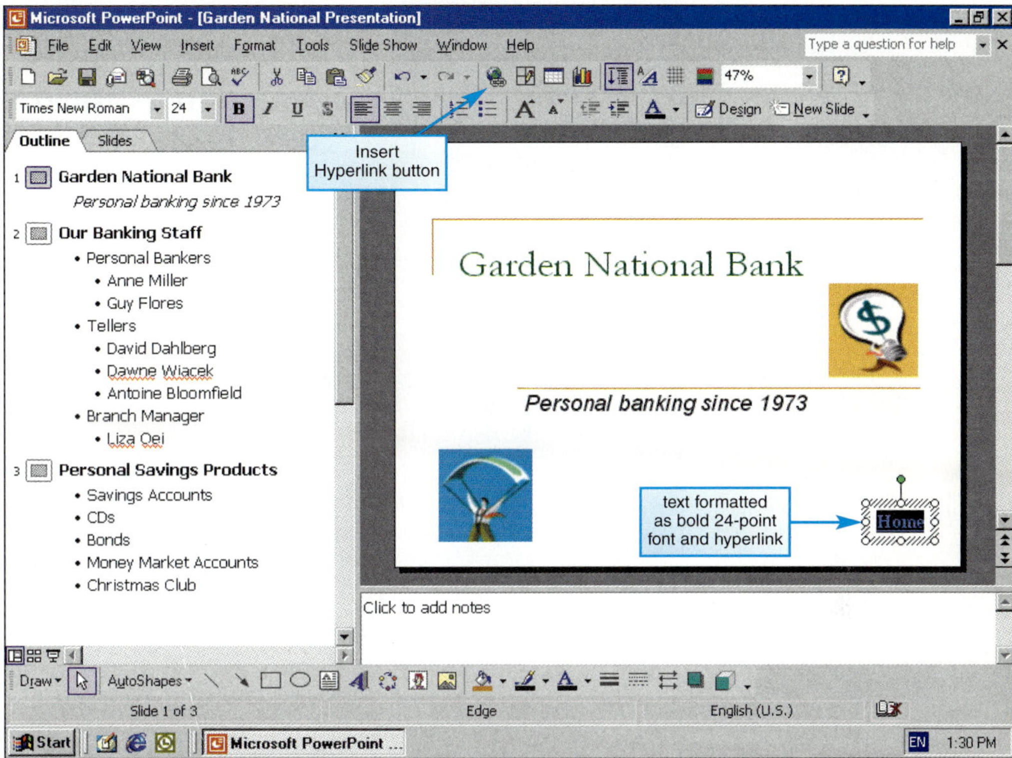

FIGURE 1-30

Other Ways

1. On Insert menu click Hyperlink
2. Right-click highlighted word, click Hyperlink on shortcut menu
3. Press CTRL+K
4. In Voice Command mode say, "Hyperlink"

Viewing and Saving the PowerPoint Web Page

Just as you did in the previous section of this project, view the Web page before saving it. It is important to verify all of the Web page navigation features before you save the file.

TO VIEW THE WEB PAGE IN YOUR BROWSER

1. Click File on the menu bar and then point to Web Page Preview.
2. Click Web Page Preview.
3. If necessary, click the Maximize button on your browser's title bar.

The PowerPoint Web page displays (Figure 1-31 on the next page).

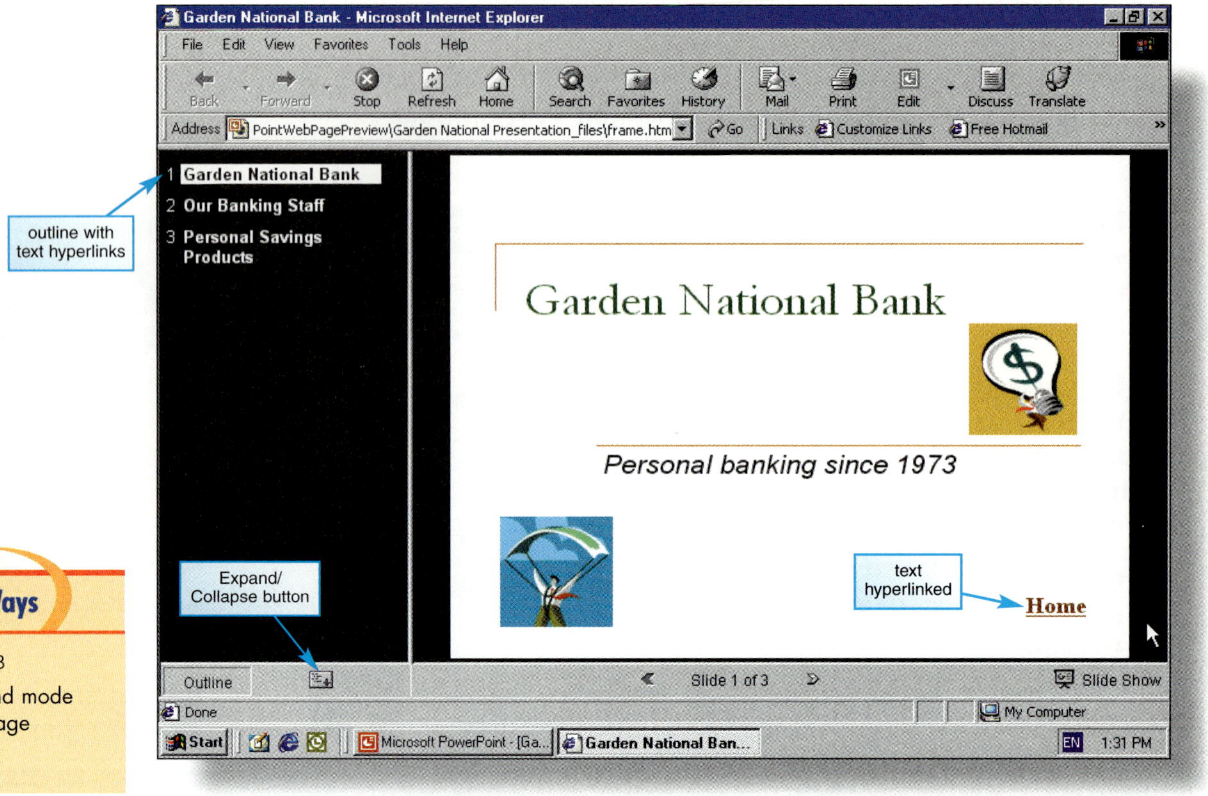

FIGURE 1-31

Other Ways

1. Press ALT+F, type B
2. In Voice Command mode say, "File, Web Page Preview"

More About

Outline

The outline pane is displayed by default when you view a presentation in a browser. To hide this pane, click the Outline button while in the browser. Click the Outline button again to redisplay the outline pane.

Slide 1 of the PowerPoint presentation Web page contains a hyperlink to the home page of the Garden National Bank Web site. Although you created this hyperlink by adding a text box to the first slide, you also can create hyperlinks from existing text or images in a PowerPoint presentation. For example, one of the logo images on slide 1 could be used as a hyperlink to the home page of the Web site. Using one of those images, however, does not give the Web page visitor a clear idea of where the hyperlink will lead. It is more appropriate to create a hyperlink to the home page from text — for example, Home — that makes sense to the visitor.

In addition to any hyperlinks that are added to the presentation, PowerPoint automatically creates hyperlinks in the left column of the Web page, called the **outline**. This outline can be expanded or collapsed using the **Expand/Collapse Outline button** below the outline pane and is used to navigate through the Web page presentation (Figure 1-31). The text in the heading of each slide is used as the phrases for these hyperlinks. When you click a link, you jump to that particular slide within the presentation. The ease of navigation within a PowerPoint Web page is valuable to the Web page visitor.

As well as being able to add your own hyperlink text, PowerPoint provides some ready-made action buttons that you can insert into your Web pages. **Action buttons** contain shapes, such as left and right arrows, that can be used to hyperlink to other Web pages within the presentation. You can insert symbols on the action buttons for going to the next (right arrow), previous (left arrow), first (beginning arrow), and last (end arrow) slides. PowerPoint also includes action buttons for playing movies or sounds. You insert these action buttons using the slide master feature of PowerPoint.

Saving the PowerPoint Presentation as a Web Page

The next step is to save the PowerPoint presentation as a Web page. When you save a PowerPoint presentation as a Web page, the Web page is saved in a default folder. All supporting files, such as backgrounds and images, are organized in this folder automatically. The name of the PowerPoint slide show opened in this section is Garden National Presentation. PowerPoint uses the name of the saved Web page and adds the string, files, for the name of the new folder. When the current presentation is saved as a Web page, the folder name that PowerPoint Web creates is AboutUs_files. The default name for the first slide in the presentation is frame.htm. The structure used in the folder organization makes Web page publishing easier because you can keep track of all of the files associated with the Web page. You also can edit the files manually, rather than using PowerPoint.

Perform the steps below to save the PowerPoint presentation as a Web page.

> **More About**
>
> **Web Page Publishing**
>
> The Web pages created in this project all are stored locally on your computer. Typically, a Web page must be published to a server inside the organization or at your ISP. Microsoft offers a Web Page Publishing Wizard to assist in moving all of the related files and directories that comprise a Web site.

TO SAVE THE POWERPOINT PRESENTATION AS A WEB PAGE

1. Click the Microsoft PowerPoint button on the taskbar.
2. Click File on the menu bar and then click Save as Web Page.
3. Type `AboutUs` in the File name text box.
4. If necessary, click the Look in box arrow and then click 3½ Floppy (A:) in the Look in list.
5. Click the Save button in the Save As dialog box.

The PowerPoint presentation is saved as a Web page.

The task of saving the PowerPoint presentation as a Web page is complete. The hyperlink has been added to the first page of the presentation that jumps to the Web site home page when clicked. Standard Web page navigation was added automatically to the presentation that allows the Web page visitor to jump to any slide in the Web page presentation. All of the files necessary for the Web page were saved in a folder named AboutUs_files.

After saving the PowerPoint presentation as a Web page, you can quit PowerPoint and close your browser as shown in the following steps.

TO QUIT POWERPOINT AND CLOSE YOUR BROWSER

1. Click the Close button on the PowerPoint title bar.
2. Click the Close button on the browser title bar.

Creating a Data Access Page from an Access Database

The next step in the Garden National Bank Web site creation is to use an Access database to create a data access page. A **data access page** is a special type of Web page that is designed for viewing and working with data. Similar to a form, a data access page is connected, or bound, directly to an Access database.

Data access pages are used to analyze data, enter and edit data, make projections, and review data. You also can create a chart using the chart component to analyze trends, show patterns, and make comparisons on the data in the database. Then, you can add spreadsheet controls to allow the inclusion of formulas for calculations.

> **More About**
>
> **Viewing Web Pages**
>
> In addition to Microsoft Windows environments, many environments exist for viewing Web pages. When creating a Web page with special features, such as data access pages, it is important to make sure that the special features are supported within the environment in which the Web page viewers operate. For example, users who view Web pages on Apple Macintosh computers may have a different Web page viewing experience.

One of the more common purposes of data access pages is for viewing records in a database via a company's intranet or the World Wide Web. Data access pages provide a method to make inquiries of large amounts of data in a selective way. Groups of records can be expanded or collapsed so that Web page visitors can view the data they want to see.

Perform the following steps to open an Access database.

TO START ACCESS AND OPEN AN EXISTING DATABASE

1. Click the Start button on the Windows taskbar. Click Open Office Document on the Start menu.
2. If necessary, click the Look in box arrow and then click 3½ Floppy (A:) in the Look in list.
3. Double-click the Garden National Bank Products database name.
4. If the Language bar displays, click its Minimize button.

Access starts and opens the Garden National Bank Products : Database window (Figure 1-32).

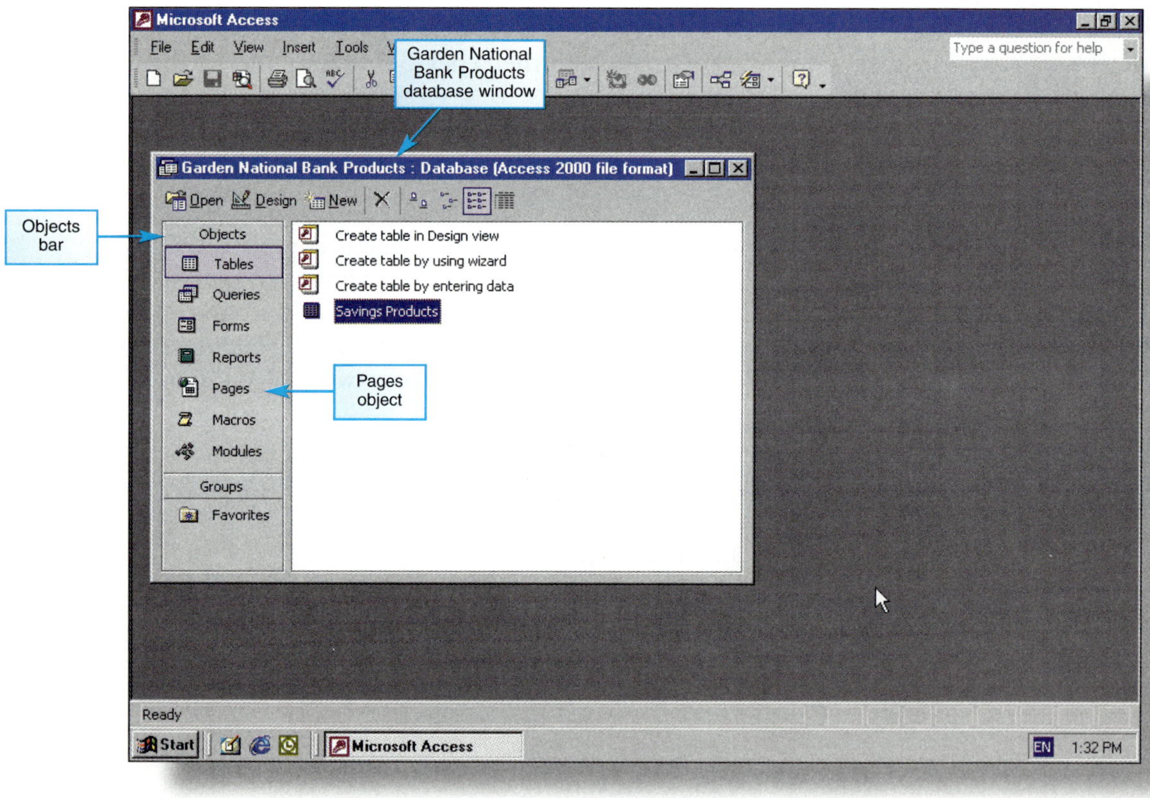

FIGURE 1-32

Creating a Data Access Page Using the Wizard

For the Garden National Bank Web site, you do not want the database to be altered by the Web page visitor in any way. The visitors should be allowed only to view the data. Because of this, you must add a group level to the data access page. Adding **group levels** results in a read-only page. The Web page visitors can view all data and alter that view, but they cannot change the data itself.

Perform the following steps to use the Page Wizard to create a data access page.

Steps To Create a Data Access Page Using the Page Wizard

1 Click the Pages object on the Objects bar.

2 Double-click the Create data access page by using wizard in the list box.

The first Page Wizard dialog box displays (Figure 1-33). The Savings Products table is selected automatically because it is the only table in the database. If more than one table exists, you would need to click the Tables object on the Objects bar and then select the appropriate table before clicking the Pages object in Step 1.

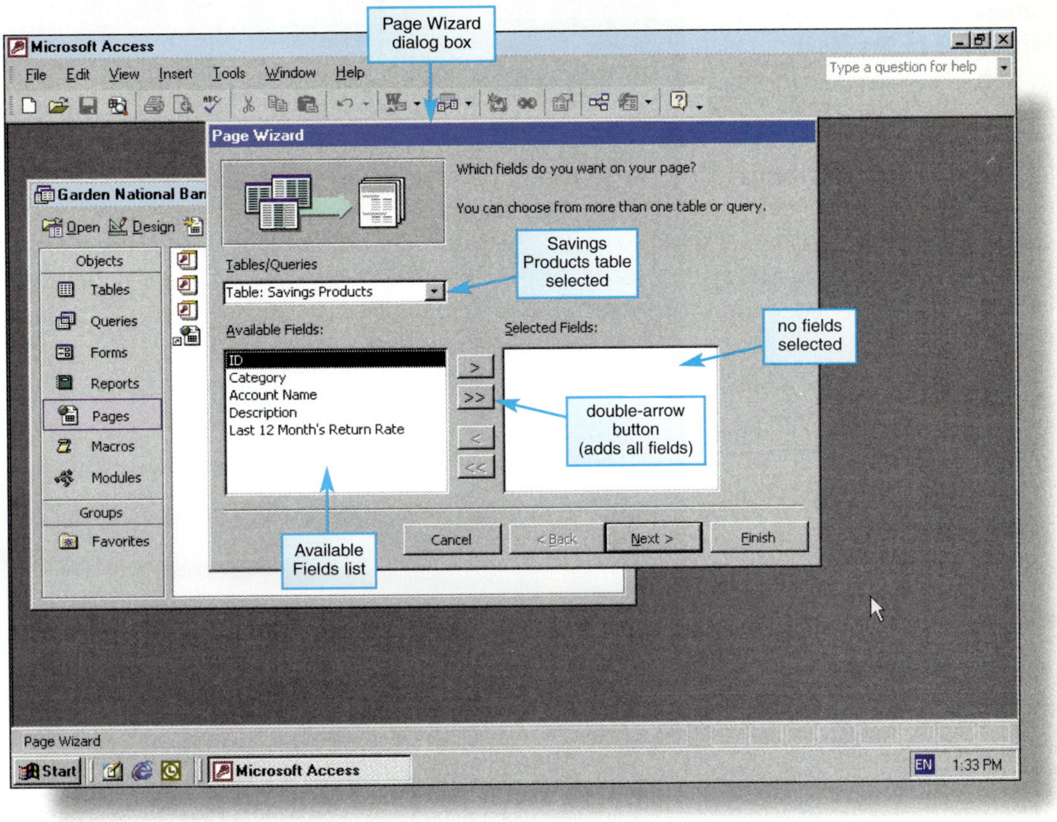

FIGURE 1-33

3 Click the double-arrow button to add all the fields. Point to the Next button.

All the fields in the table are listed in the Selected Fields list (Figure 1-34). This means you want to display all the fields on the data access page.

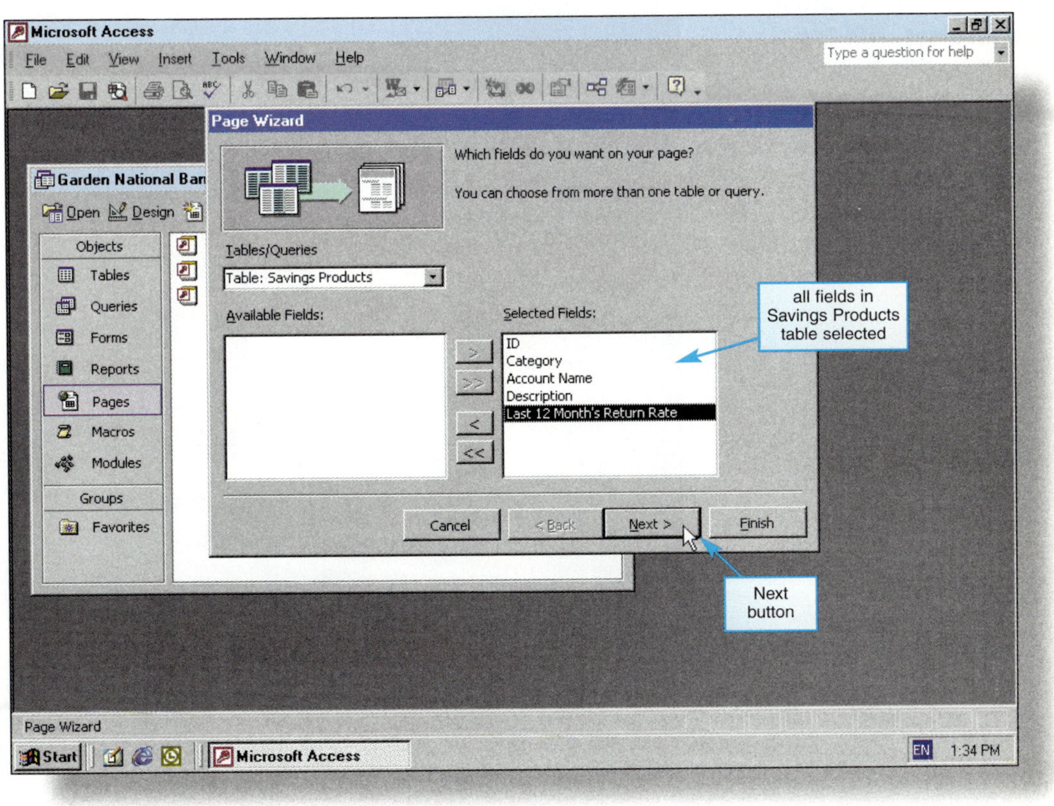

FIGURE 1-34

4 **Click the Next button. Double-click Category in the box on the left. Point to the Next button.**

Adding a group level, such as Category, prohibits the data access page from being updated. Category displays in the upper-right box indicating it has been selected (Figure 1-35).

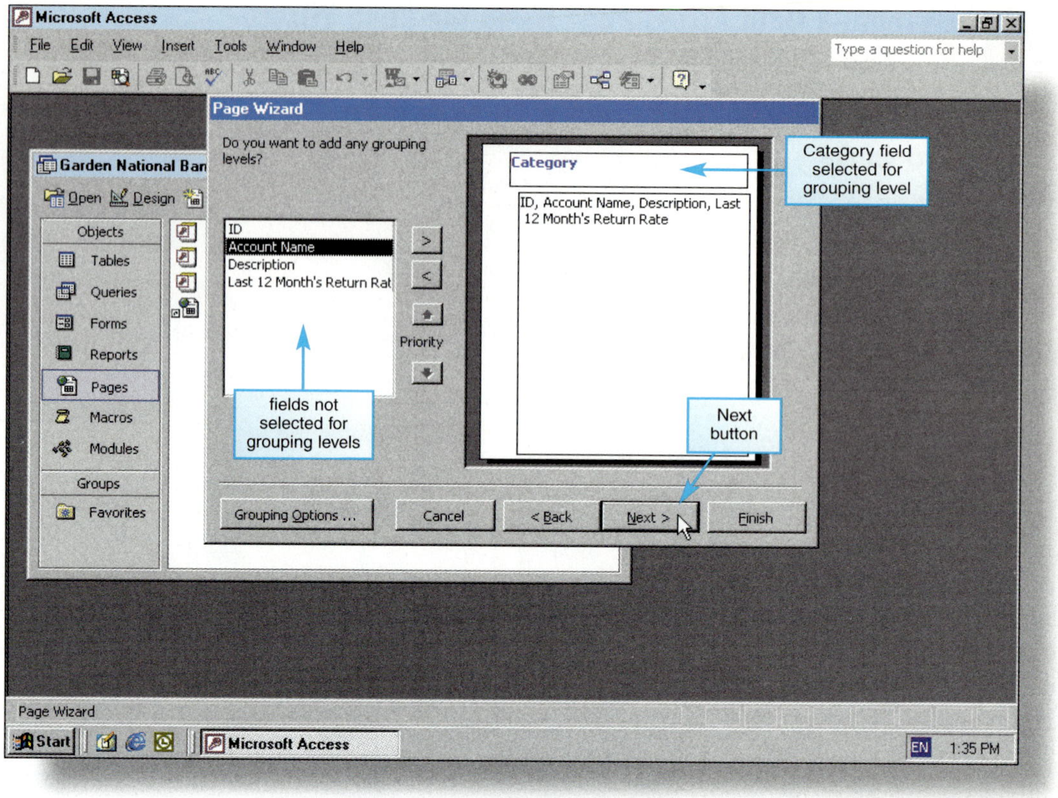

FIGURE 1-35

5 **Click the Next button. When the next Page Wizard dialog box displays with the question, What sort order do you want for your records?, point to the Next button.**

The next Page Wizard dialog box displays (Figure 1-36).

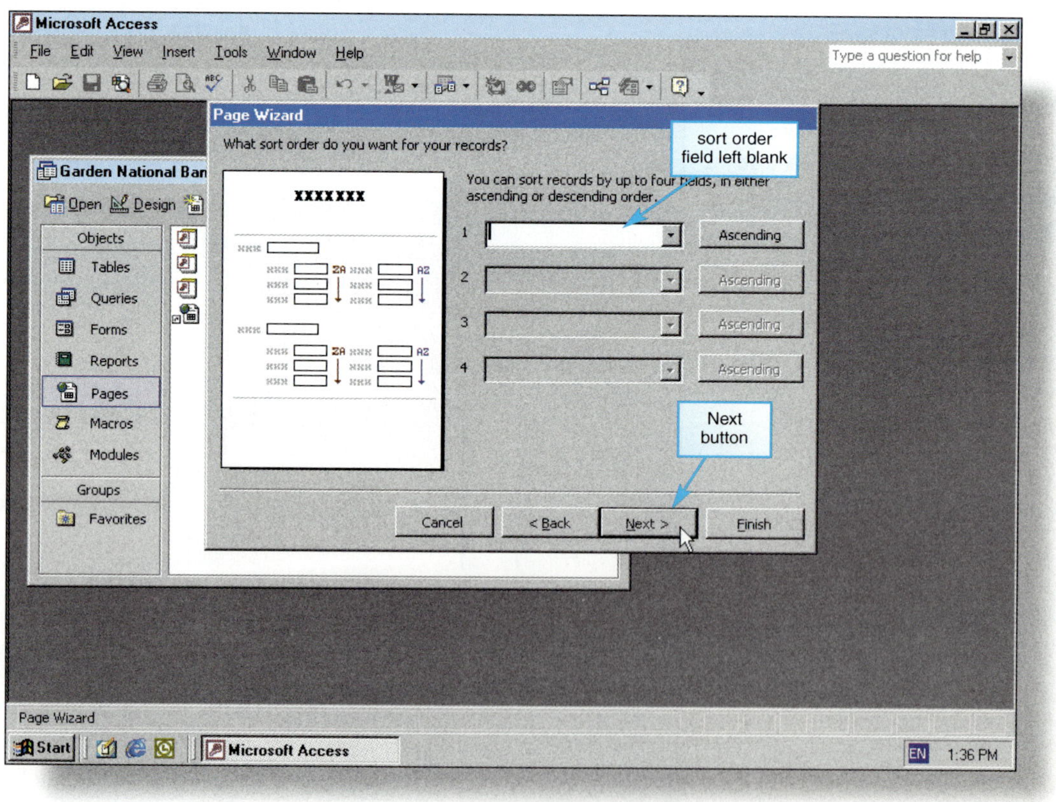

FIGURE 1-36

6 **Click the Next button and then type** Savings Products **in the What title do you want for your page? text box. If necessary, click Modify the page's design to select it. Point to the Finish button.**

The next Page Wizard dialog box displays with the title, Savings Products, in the text box and the Modify the page's design option button selected (Figure 1-37).

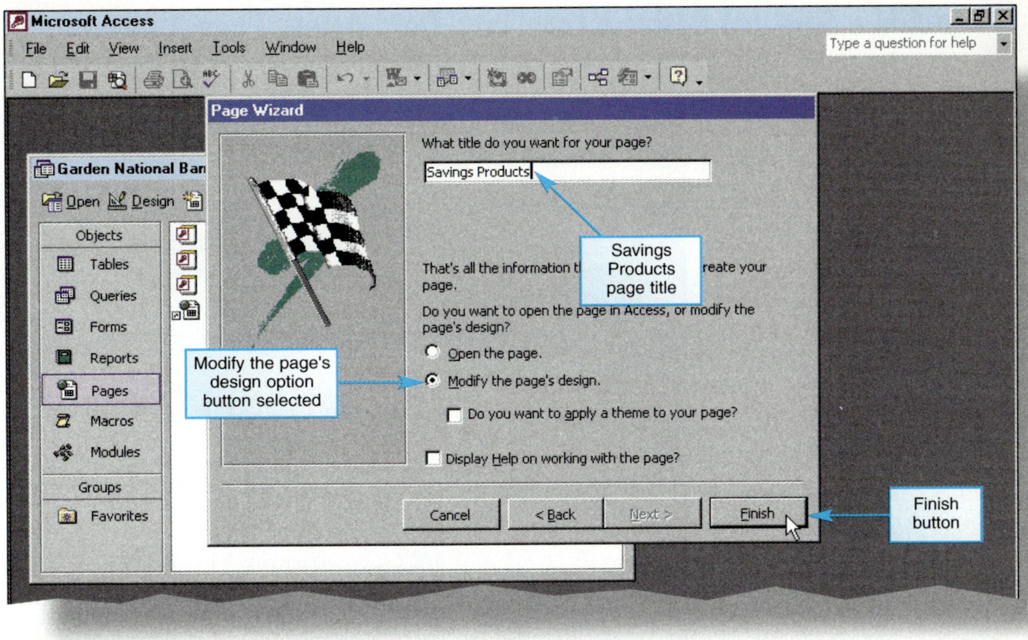

FIGURE 1-37

7 **Click the Finish button. If necessary, close the Field List Pane.**

Access displays the data access page in Design view (Figure 1-38).

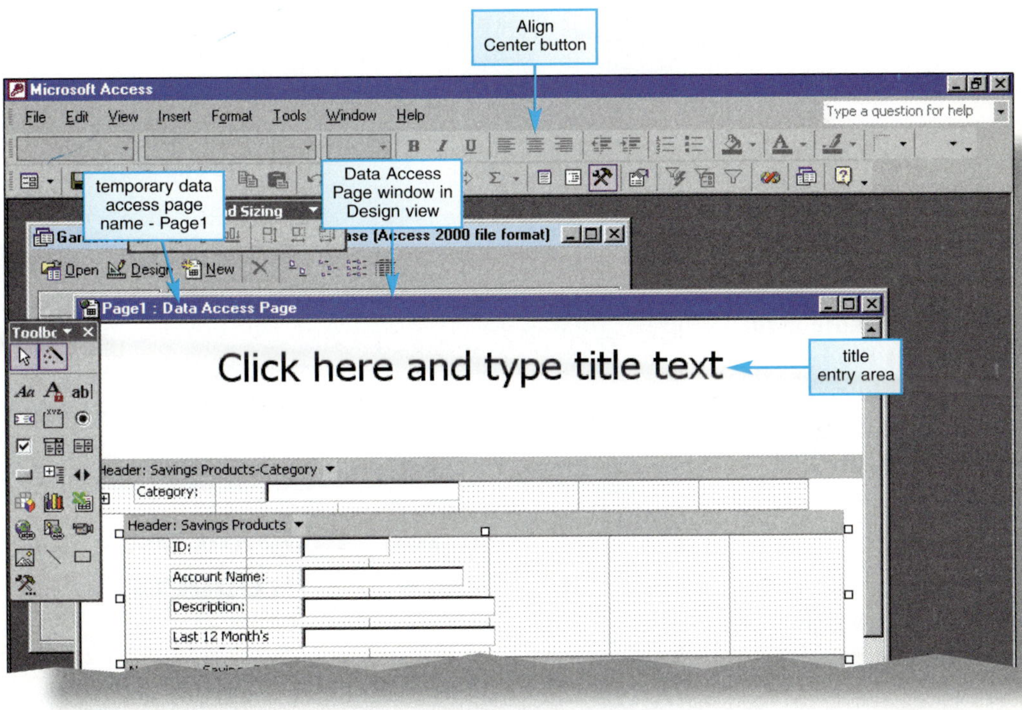

FIGURE 1-38

Adding a Title and Resizing a Label on a Data Access Page

The data access page is created, but additional information can be helpful for the Web page visitor. It is customary to insert a title at the top of the page that tells the visitor the purpose of the Web page. Resizing the Last 12 Month's Return Rate is necessary because the entire text of the label does not show after completing the Data Access Page Wizard. The steps on the next page explain how to add a title and resize a label.

Steps To Add a Title and Resize a Label on a Data Access Page

1 **If necessary, scroll to the top of the data access page. With the data access page in Design view, click anywhere in the Click here and type title text entry area. Type** `Garden National Bank Savings Products` **as the title.**

The data access page displays as shown in Figure 1-39.

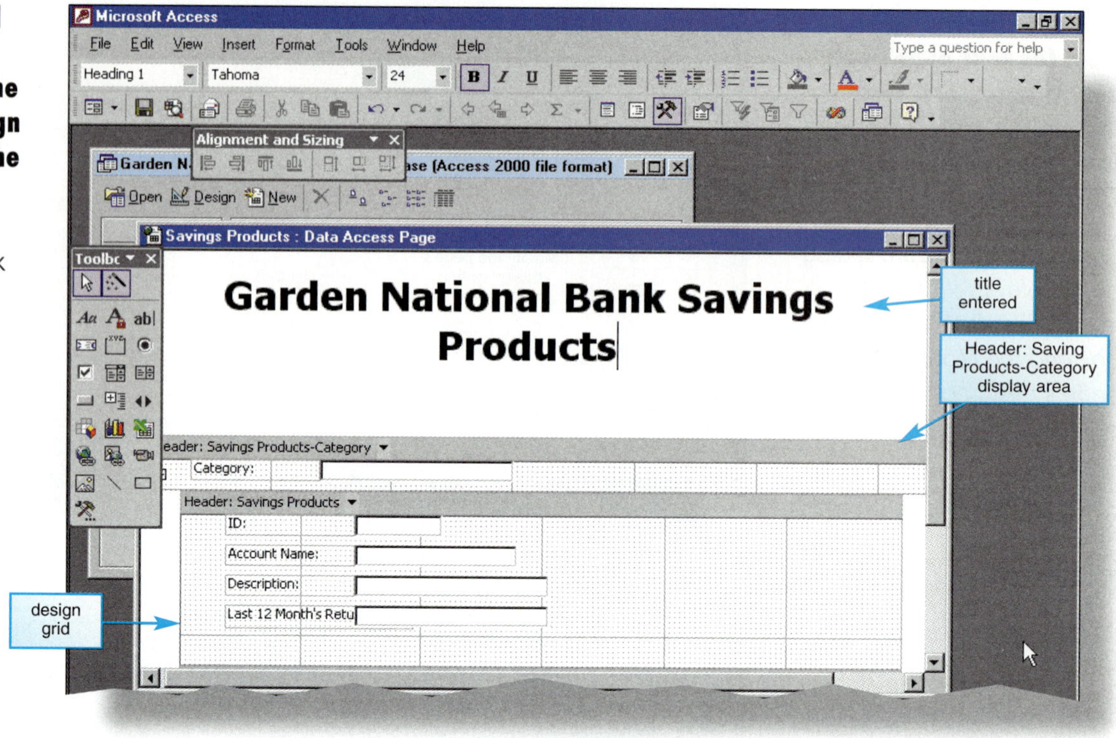

FIGURE 1-39

2 **Click anywhere within the Last 12 Month's Return Rate label in the Savings Products area of the data access page to select the label. Point to the lower-right sizing handle on the label.**

3 **Drag the resize handle straight down so that it doubles in height.**

4 **Release the mouse button.**

The Last 12 Month's Return Rate label is resized, and the data access page displays as shown in Figure 1-40.

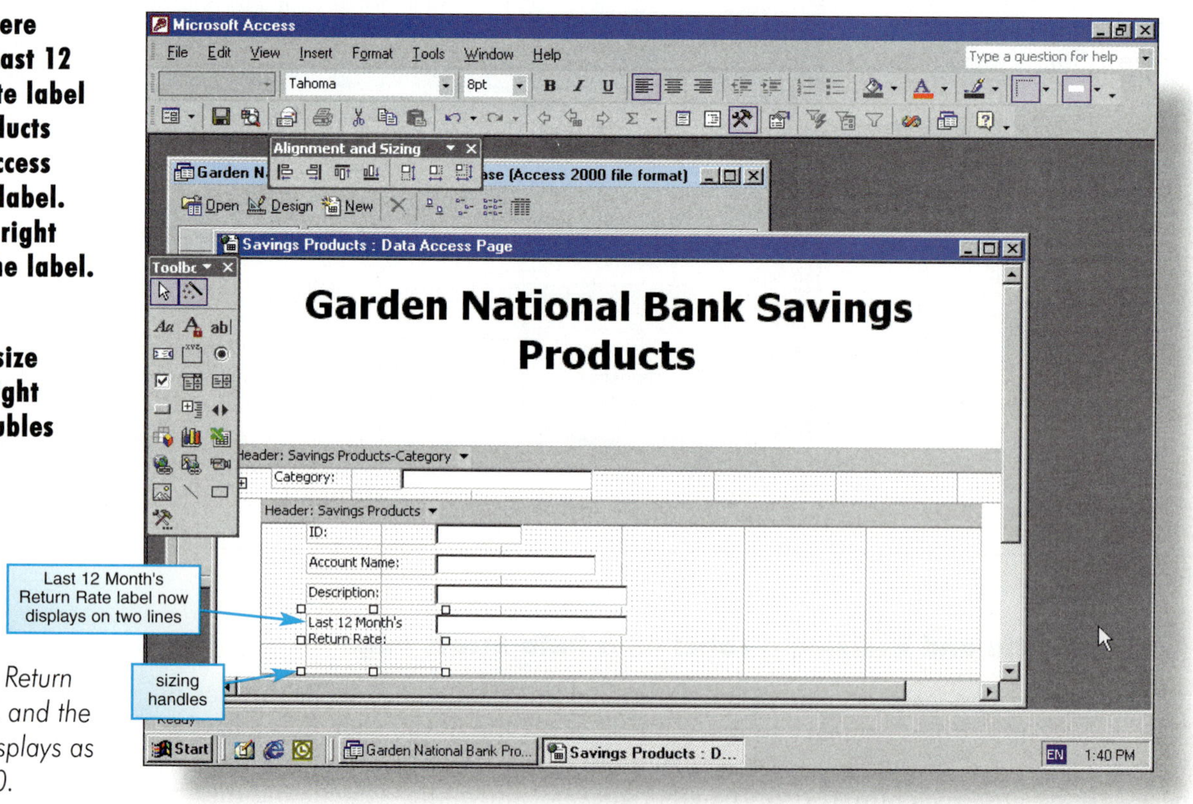

FIGURE 1-40

The data access page is created, a heading is positioned in the header, and the label is resized as shown in Figure 1-1d on page I 1.06. The next step is to add a hyperlink that returns the visitor to the Web site home page.

More About

Data Access Pages

In addition to using Data access pages in a browser, you also can work with a data access page in Page view in Microsoft Access. Data access pages can supplement the forms and reports that you use in your database application. When deciding whether to design a data access page, form, or report, consider the tasks you want to perform.

Adding a Hyperlink to a Data Access Page

Just as you did on the PowerPoint Web page, a hyperlink to the home page should be added to the data access page. This allows the Web page visitor to return to the Garden National Bank home page without having to repeatedly click the Back button on the browser's toolbar. Perform the following steps to add a hyperlink to the data access page.

Steps To Add a Hyperlink into a Data Access Page

1 If necessary, click View on the menu bar and then click Toolbox to display the Toolbox. Scroll down so the bottom of the data access page displays. Click the Hyperlink button on the Toolbox and then point below the Design grid.

The hyperlink mouse pointer displays as shown in Figure 1-41.

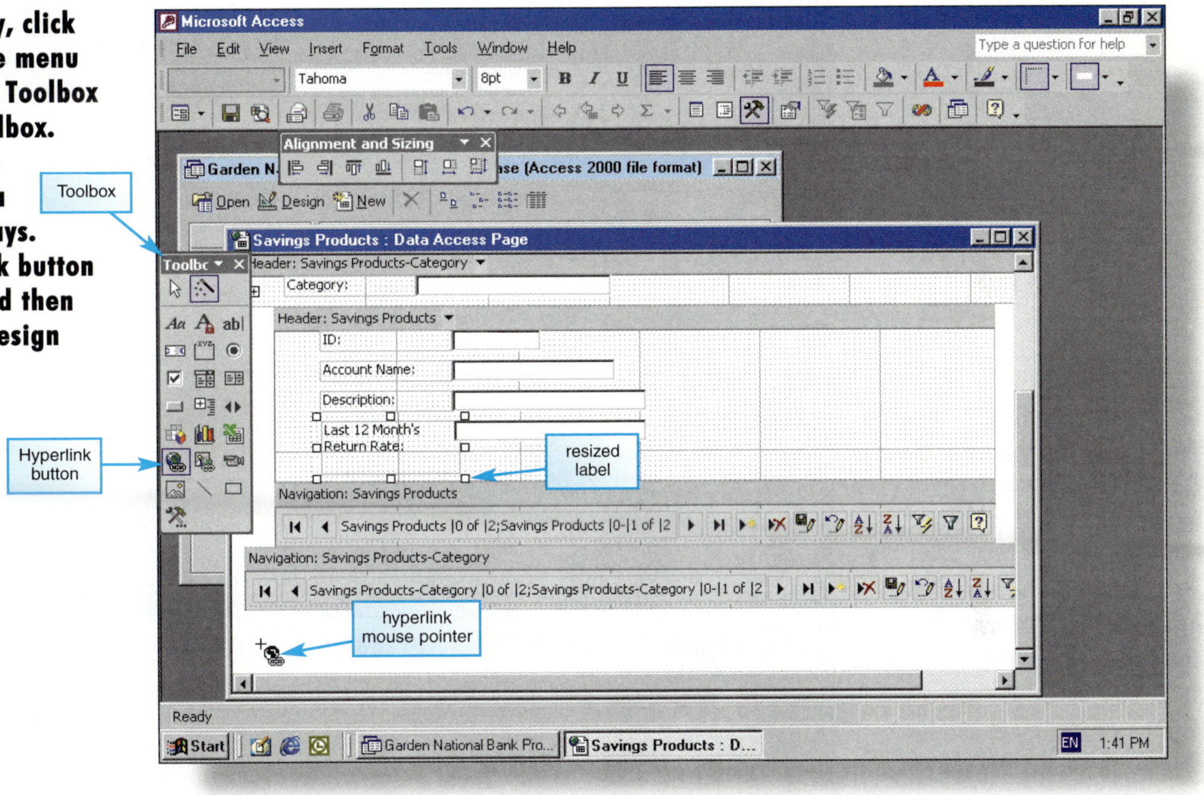

FIGURE 1-41

2 **Click below the Design grid.**

The Insert Hyperlink dialog box displays (Figure 1-42).

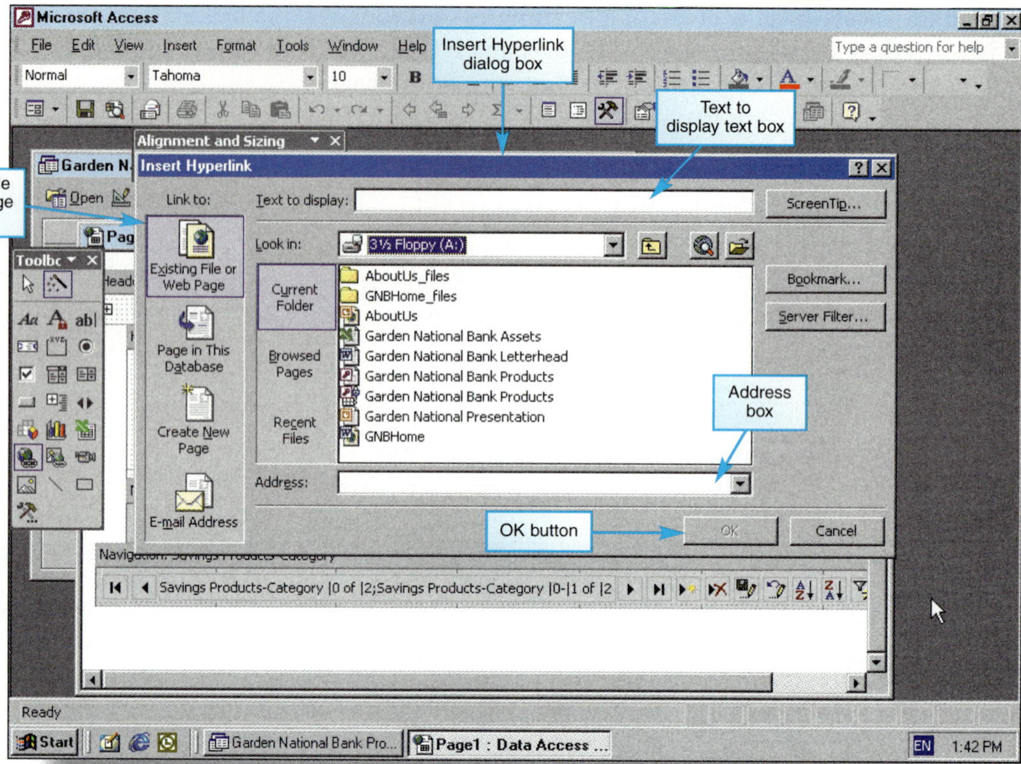

FIGURE 1-42

3 **If necessary, click the Existing File or Web Page button on the Link to bar. Type** `Home` **in the Text to display text box. Type** `a:\GNBHome.htm` **in the Address text box and then click the OK button.**

4 **Click anywhere on the data access page to deselect the hyperlink box.**

The data access page displays as shown in Figure 1-43.

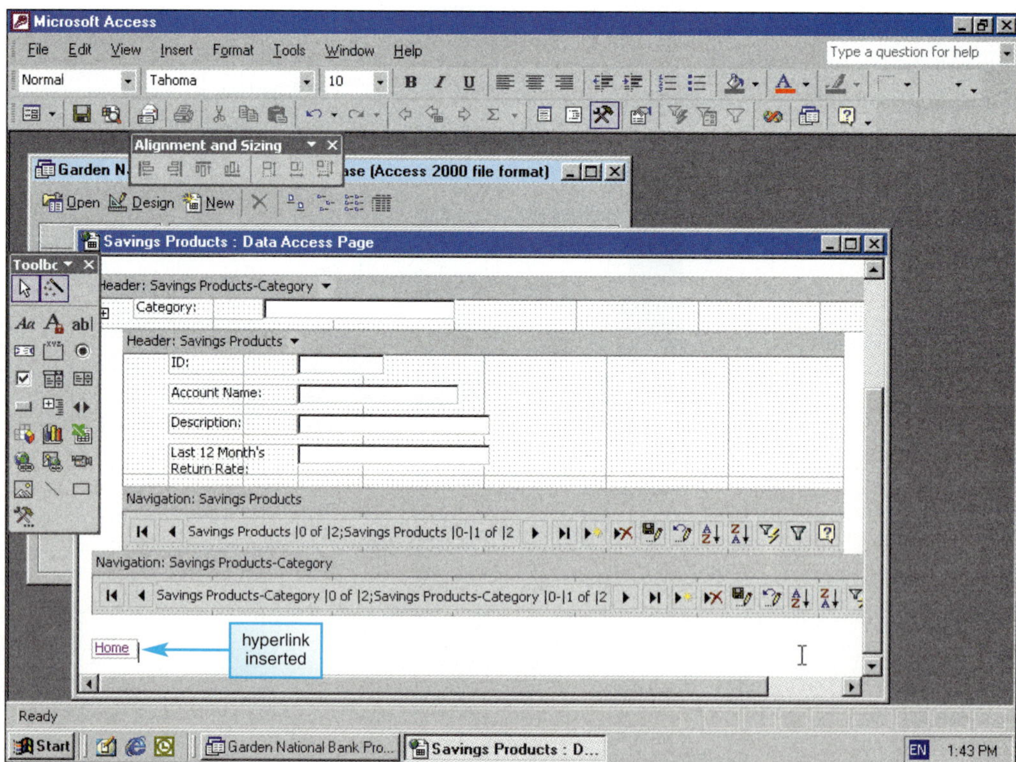

FIGURE 1-43

Other Ways

1. Right-click below Design grid, and in Voice Command mode say, "Hyperlink"

The data access page is complete. In the next section, you will save the page to the Integration Data Disk and view it in the browser.

Saving the Data Access Page and Viewing It

In other sections of this project, you have viewed the Web page, verified that it is correct, and then saved it on a floppy disk. Unlike Word and PowerPoint, you must save a data access page before you can preview it in your browser. As the Web page is being opened in your browser, a Databinding message displays on the status bar of your browser. This indicates that the data access page is connecting to the database that was open when the page was created (Garden National Bank Products).

Perform the following steps to save the file on the Integration Data Disk and then view it in your browser.

More About

Database Connections

When a Web page tries to obtain data from a database, such as Access, you must be sure that the database is accessible to the Web page. When publishing Web pages that include Data access pages, you should check with your system administrator to make sure that the Web page will have the proper access to the database.

TO SAVE THE DATA ACCESS PAGE AND VIEW IT IN YOUR BROWSER

1. Click File on the menu bar and then click Web Page Preview. When the Microsoft Access dialog box displays, click the Yes button.
2. When the Save As Data Access Page dialog box displays, type `SavingsProducts` in the File name text box. If necessary, click 3½ Floppy (A:) in the Look in list.
3. Click the Save button in the Save As Data Access Page dialog box.
4. Click the Expand indicator to the left of the GroupOfProducts-Category to expand the display.

The data access page displays in your browser (Figure 1-44).

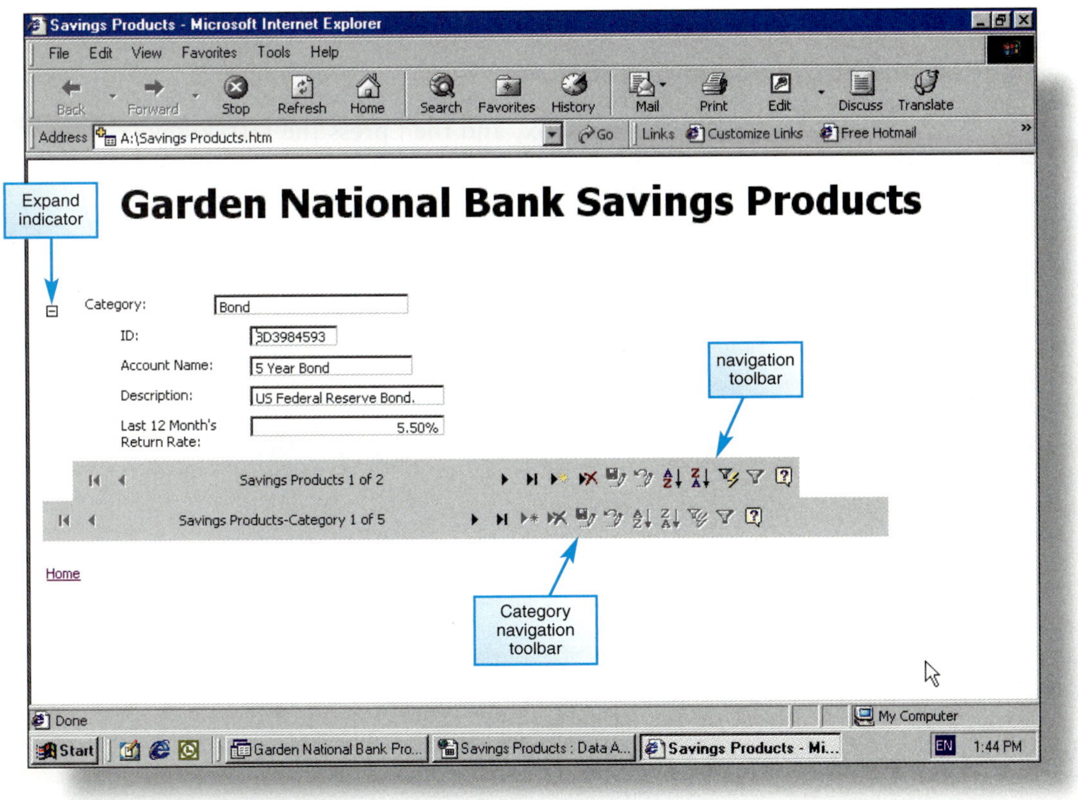

FIGURE 1-44

Once the data access page is saved, you can preview it and then quit Access and close your browser, as shown in the following steps.

TO QUIT ACCESS AND CLOSE YOUR BROWSER

1. Right-click the Garden National Bank Products button on the taskbar and then click Close on the shortcut menu.
2. Click the Close button on the Access title bar to quit Access.

Grouping records on a data access page is similar to grouping records on a report. You can group the data on this data access page in different ways, but the user cannot edit the data. The records in the data access page can be expanded or collapsed, using the Expand and Collapse indicators. This allows users to customize their view of the data and remove extra data from view that may not interest them. Using the **navigation toolbars** on the data access page, you can move, sort, and filter records and obtain Help.

Use the navigation toolbar to verify that the information in the database displays correctly. Click the link to the home page of the Web site to verify it.

More About

Microsoft Certification

The Microsoft Office User Specialist (MOUS) Certification program provides an opportunity for you to obtain a valuable industry credential — proof that you have the Office XP skills required by employers. For more information, see Appendix E or visit the Shelly Cashman Series MOUS Web page at scsite.com/offxp/cert.htm.

Testing the Web Site

The Garden National Bank Web site is complete. To ensure that all the links in the Web site are viable, perform the following steps to open the home page and then thoroughly test the entire Web site.

TO TEST THE WEB SITE

1. Start your browser.
2. Click the Address bar of your browser.
3. Type `a:\GNBHome.htm` in the text box, and then press the ENTER key.

The home page of the Garden National Bank Web site displays as shown in Figure 1-45.

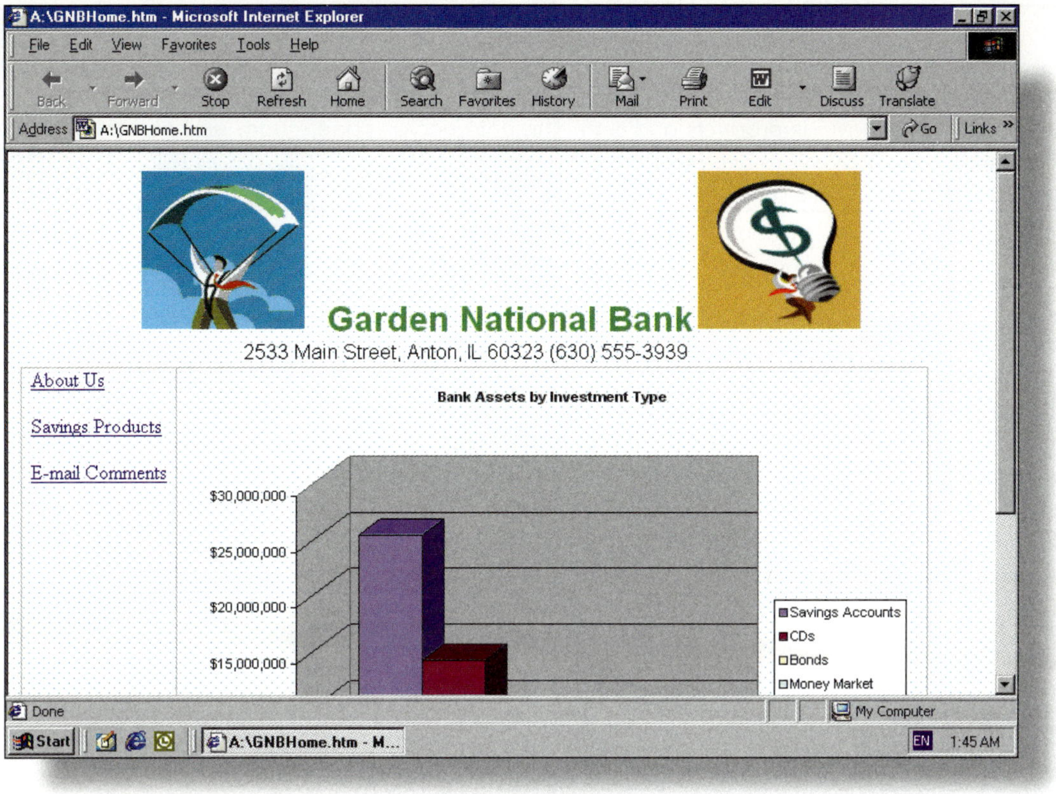

FIGURE 1-45

Verifying the Hyperlinks in Your Browser

All hyperlinks should be tested by clicking them and verifying that they jump to the correct Web page. Three hyperlinks are on the home page: About Us, Savings Products, and E-mail Comments. Perform the following steps to test the links.

TO VERIFY THE HYPERLINKS

1. Click the About Us hyperlink.
2. Click the navigation buttons to view all slides on the Web page.
3. On the first slide on the PowerPoint Web page, click the Home hyperlink.
4. Click the Savings Products hyperlink. Click the Expand and Collapse indicators and then scroll through the database using the navigation toolbars.
5. On the data access page, click the Home hyperlink.
6. Click the E-mail Comments hyperlink.

A new e-mail message displays with manager@isp.com in the To text box.

With the hyperlinks verified, follow these steps to quit the e-mail program and your browser.

TO QUIT E-MAIL AND CLOSE YOUR BROWSER

1. Click the Close button on your e-mail program.
2. Click the Close button on your browser's title bar.

More About

Discussions

The Discussions feature enables you and other people to insert remarks into a Web page. The discussions are threaded; that is, replies to a discussion remark are nested directly below it. You can have multiple discussions in progress simultaneously. You start a discussion from within your browser. The Discussions feature is available only with Microsoft Office Server Extensions, a feature that is set up by a system administrator on a server. Learn more about Discussions in Word Help.

CASE PERSPECTIVE SUMMARY

Liza is very pleased with the new Web site that you helped her create. She thinks it will better educate the community on the benefits of Garden National Bank's savings products and staff. The data access page, chart, and presentation can easily be updated with current information. Now Liza feels better prepared to compete.

Project Summary

This project introduced you to integrating Microsoft Office XP applications. You started this project by opening an existing Word document and creating a two-column, one-row, borderless table. You then inserted three hyperlinks and embedded a Bar chart from an existing Excel worksheet. You saved that document as an HTML file. You then opened an existing PowerPoint presentation and added a hyperlink to the first slide. You saved this presentation as a Web page. Finally, you opened an existing Access database. You used the Page Wizard to create a data access page from that database. You created a group level so that the database could be viewed but not changed. You saved that data access page and viewed and tested all Web pages and hyperlinks in your browser.

What You Should Know

Having completed this project, you now should be able to perform the following tasks.

- Add a Hyperlink into a Data Access Page *(I 1.37)*
- Add a Title and Resize a Label on a Data Access Page *(I 1.36)*
- Add Text for a Hyperlink into a PowerPoint Presentation *(I 1.28)*
- Change the Size of an Embedded Object *(I 1.17)*
- Create a Data Access Page Using the Page Wizard *(I 1.33)*
- Create a Hyperlink to PowerPoint Web Pages *(I 1.12)*
- Display the Web Tools Toolbar *(I 1.20)*
- Embed an Excel Chart into a Word Document *(I 1.14)*
- Insert a Hyperlink into a PowerPoint Presentation *(I 1.29)*
- Insert a Table into a Word Document *(I 1.09)*
- Insert Scrolling Text into a Word Document *(I 1.21)*
- Insert Text for Hyperlinks *(I 1.11)*
- Insert the Remaining Hyperlinks *(I 1.13)*
- Preview the Web Page *(I 1.25)*
- Quit Access and Close Your Browser *(I 1.40)*
- Quit E-mail and Close Your Browser *(I 1.41)*
- Quit Excel *(I 1.19)*
- Quit PowerPoint and Close Your Browser *(I 1.31)*
- Quit Word *(I 1.26)*
- Remove the Table Border *(I 1.10)*
- Resize the Scrolling Text *(I 1.23)*
- Save a Document with a New File Name *(I 1.25)*
- Save the Data Access Page and View It in Your Browser *(I 1.39)*
- Save the PowerPoint Presentation as a Web Page *(I 1.31)*
- Start Access and Open an Existing Database *(I 1.32)*
- Start Excel, Customize Excel, and Open an Existing Workbook *(I 1.14)*
- Start PowerPoint, Customize Powerpoint, and Open an Existing Presentation *(I 1.27)*
- Start Word, Customize Word, Open an Existing Document, and Save the Document with Another Name *(I 1.28)*
- Test the Web Site *(I 1.40)*
- Verify the Hyperlinks *(I 1.41)*
- View the Web Page in Your Browser *(I 1.29)*

In the Lab

1 Creating a Web Page in Word with an Embedded Excel Chart

Problem: As an accountant for Baskin's Heating and Cooling, you have created a worksheet and chart in Excel to analyze the expenses for the past quarter. Create a Web page in Word and embed the chart from the Baskin's Heating and Cooling workbook on the home page. Add a link to a second Web page and an e-mail link to baskinsaccounting@isp.com below the chart. Create a second Web page in Word by embedding the Baskin's Heating and Cooling worksheet.

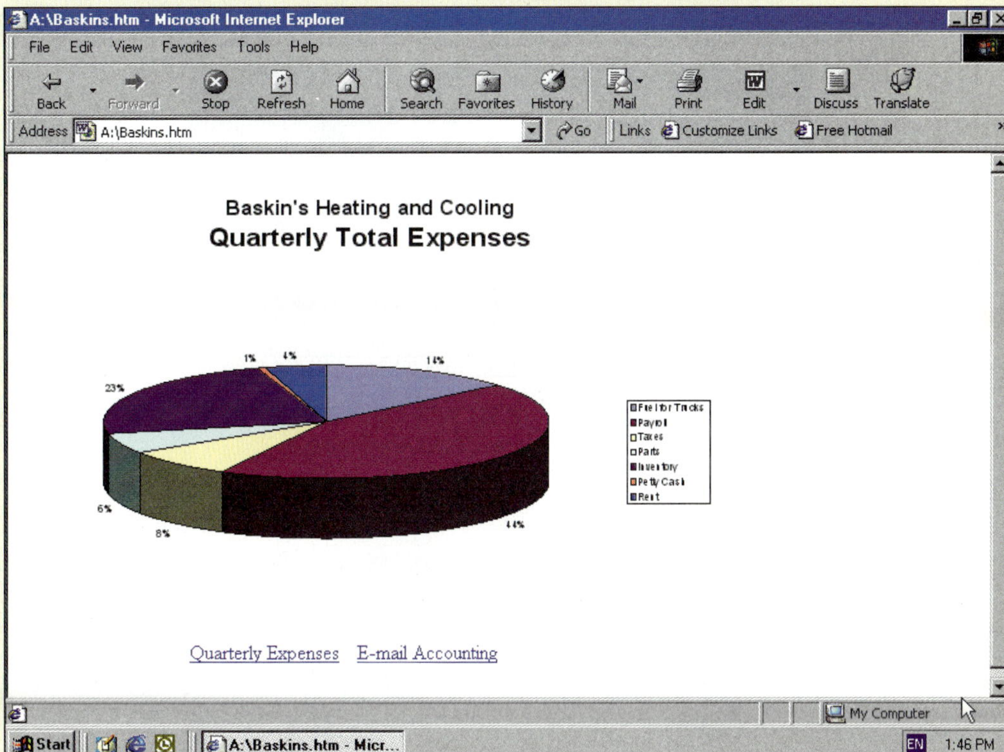

FIGURE 1-46

Instructions: Perform the following tasks.

1. Start Excel by opening the Baskin's Heating and Cooling workbook.
2. Start Word and create a new Web page. Add a title as shown in Figure 1-46. Select the Baskin's Heating and Cooling chart, copy it, and use the Paste Special dialog box in Word to embed the Excel Chart Object.
3. Add two hyperlinks to the bottom of the page in a centered, borderless table. The first hyperlink should jump to the Web page BaskinsExpense.htm, which is created next. The second hyperlink creates an e-mail to baskinsaccounting@isp.com.
4. Save this file as Baskins.htm.
5. Create a new Web page in Word.
6. Embed the Excel worksheet into the Word page. That is, switch to Excel, select the worksheet, copy the worksheet to the Clipboard, switch to Word, and use the Paste Special command on the Edit menu in Word to embed the Excel Worksheet Object.
7. Save this file as BaskinsExpense.htm.
8. View the Baskins.htm file in your browser (Figure 1-46). Print the Web page. Link to the BaskinsExpense.htm page (Figure 1-47 on the next page) and print it.

(continued)

In the Lab

Creating a Web Page in Word with an Embedded Excel Chart *(continued)*

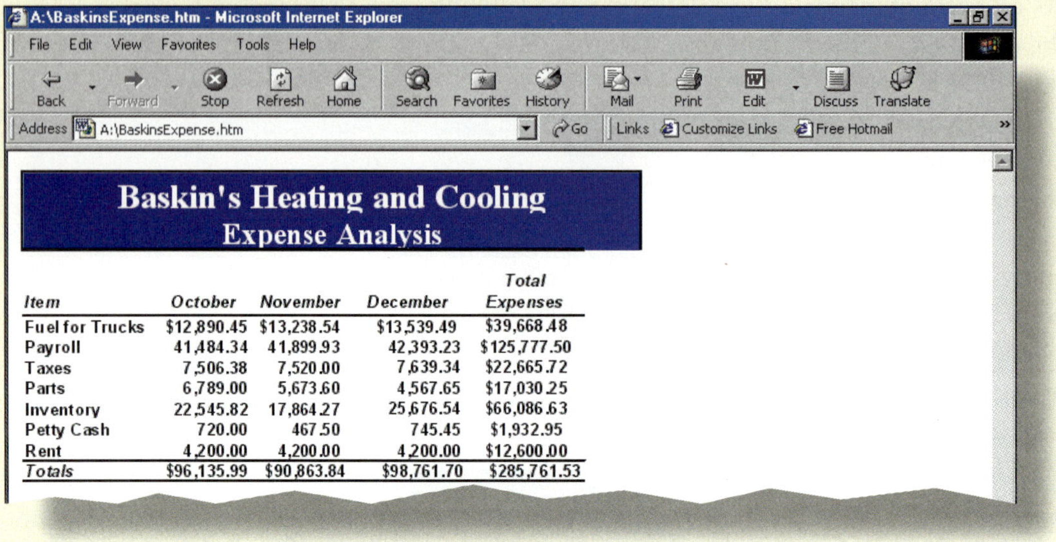

Item	October	November	December	Total Expenses
Fuel for Trucks	$12,890.45	$13,238.54	$13,539.49	$39,668.48
Payroll	41,484.34	41,899.93	42,393.23	$125,777.50
Taxes	7,506.38	7,520.00	7,639.34	$22,665.72
Parts	6,789.00	5,673.60	4,567.65	$17,030.25
Inventory	22,545.82	17,864.27	25,676.54	$66,086.63
Petty Cash	720.00	467.50	745.45	$1,932.95
Rent	4,200.00	4,200.00	4,200.00	$12,600.00
Totals	$96,135.99	$90,863.84	$98,761.70	$285,761.53

FIGURE 1-47

2 Lightning Software Web Site with Data Access Page and Excel Worksheet

Problem: As the manager of Information Technology at Lightning Software, Arthur Bukiet is responsible for loaning laptop computers to those employees who need them on a temporary basis. He would like you to design a site that allows employees to view the availability of laptop computers in inventory. He also wants an e-mail link for questions.

Instructions: Perform the following tasks.

1. Start Word. Create a home page for the Information Technology Department Laptop Loan Program Web site (Figure 1-48). Add a title and a borderless table below the title. In the left column, insert three hyperlinks. The first hyperlink should go to LightningInventory.htm (Lightning Laptops, Figure 1-49). The second hyperlink should go to LightningAvailable.htm (Laptops Available, Figure 1-50 on page I 1.46). The third hyperlink should start an e-mail to `laptop@isp.com`. Type the text in the right column. Save the Web page as LightningLaptops.htm.
2. Start Access by opening the Lightning Inventory.mdb database on the Integration Data Disk. Create a data access page from the Laptop Inventory table. Create a group level using the Operating System field. Add a title as shown in Figure 1-49. Add a link named Home that links to the LightningLaptops.htm home page at the bottom of the data access page. Save the data access page as LightningInventory.htm.
3. Start Excel by opening the Lightning Availability.xls workbook on the Integration Data Disk. Create a Web page from the workbook by using the Save as a Web Page command on the File menu. Use the file name, LightningAvailable.htm.
4. View the LightningLaptops.htm Web page in your browser. Verify that all links operate properly by clicking each one. Print all Web pages.

In the Lab

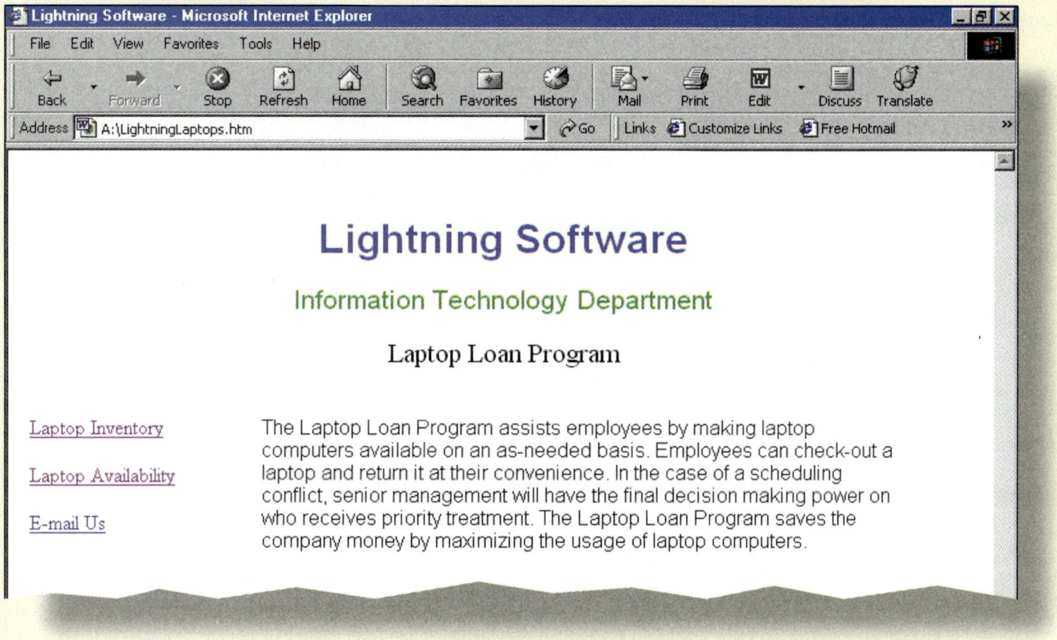

FIGURE 1-48

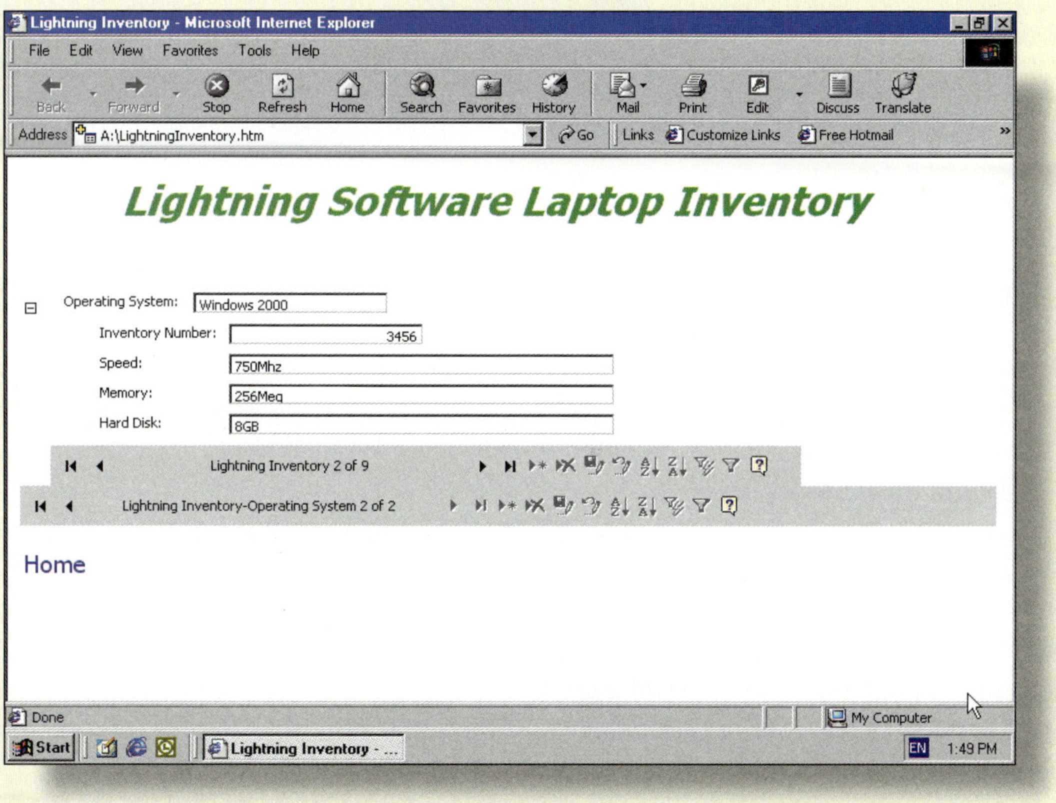

FIGURE 1-49

(continued)

In the Lab

Lightning Software Web Site with Data Access Page and Excel Worksheet *(continued)*

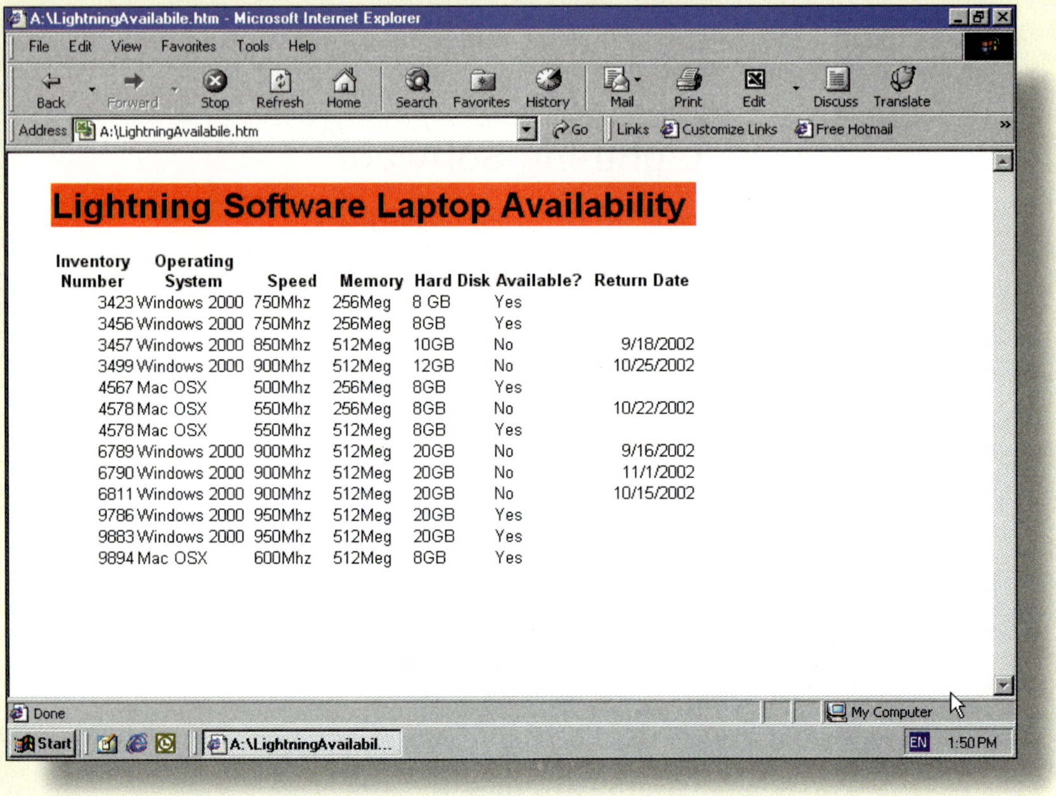

FIGURE 1-50

3 Sales Meeting Information Web Site Incorporating PowerPoint Web Pages

Problem: As sales manager for Dahlberg Office Supplies, you wish to create a Web page that promotes an upcoming meeting to all of the sales force in the company (Figures 1-51 and 1-52). The specific information for the meeting is located in a PowerPoint presentation, which has four pages.

Instructions: Perform the following tasks.

1. Start Word. Create the Web page as shown in Figure 1-51. Include scrolling text below the Web page title. Insert two hyperlinks. The first hyperlink should link to DahlbergSalesPresentation.htm, and the second should link to an e-mail address at salesmanager@isp.com. Save this Web page as DahlbergSales.htm.
2. Open the PowerPoint presentation Dahlberg.ppt. Add a link named Home at the bottom of the first page of the presentation that jumps to the DahlbergSales.htm Web page. Save the PowerPoint presentation as Web pages on the Integration Data Disk. Name the Web pages DahlbergSalesPresentation.htm.
3. View the Web pages in your browser. Print each page.

In the Lab

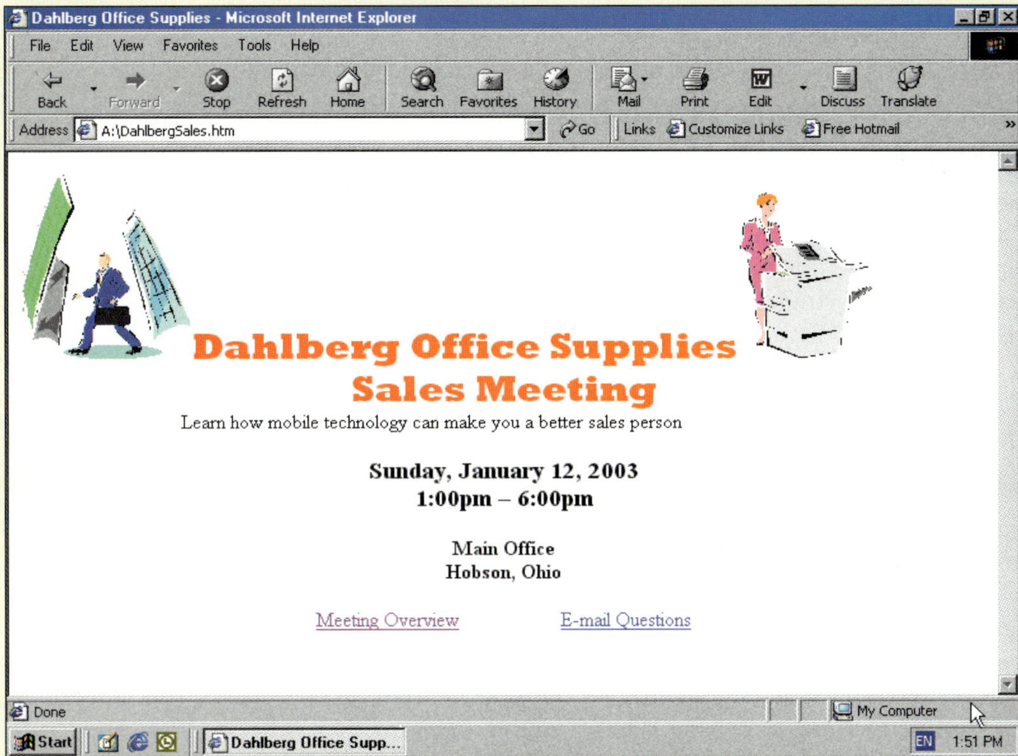

FIGURE 1-51

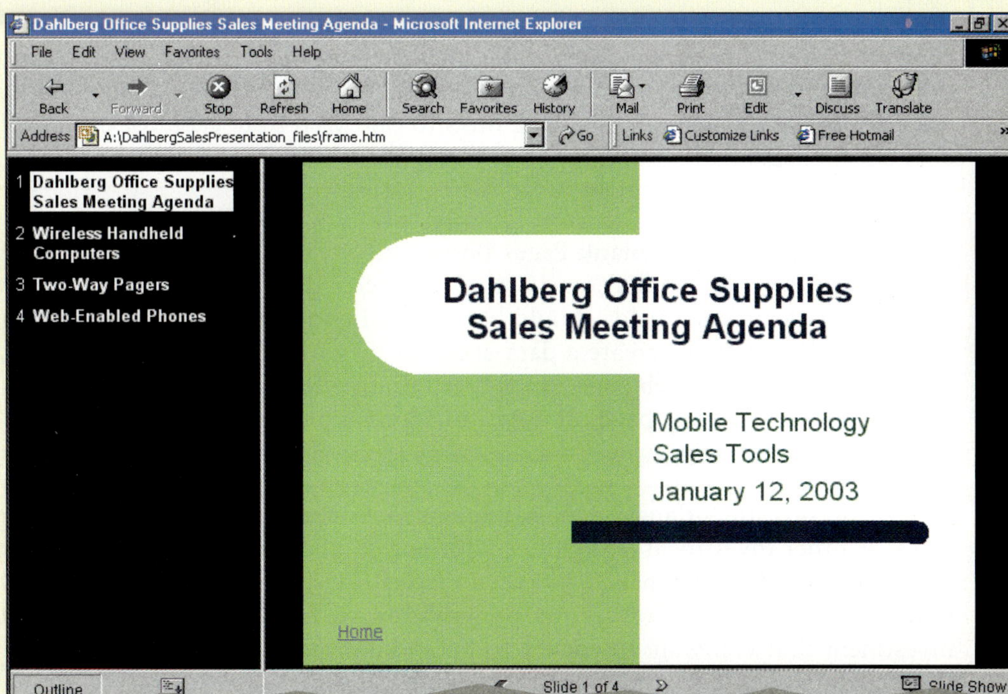

FIGURE 1-52

Cases and Places

The difficulty of these case studies varies:
◗ are the least difficult; ◗◗ are more difficult; and ◗◗◗ are the most difficult.

1 ◗ As a volunteer in your school's fund-raising department, you have been asked to create a Web page that shows the different levels of memberships for alumni donations. The membership levels have varying degrees of recognition and rewards. The Founder's Club ($1,000 and above) recognizes donors on a special plaque in the Student Union. The President's Club ($500 to $999) allows donors to have the first chance to purchase premier seats for sporting events. The Executive Club ($100 to $499) allows donors to have special parking privileges at sporting events. The Associate's Club ($10 to $99) recognizes the donors in a yearly Alumni Magazine. Create a worksheet in Excel that summarizes each of these donation levels. Create a Web page using Word that embeds the Excel worksheet; the goal of the Web site is to entice new donors to higher donation levels. Make sure an e-mail address is included on the Web page.

2 ◗ As a member of a mentoring association for local teens, you have been tasked with consolidating information about local colleges for the teens. Research the programs and accreditations of local colleges and determine the following for each: name, location, phone number for admissions office, size of student body, overview of degree types offered, and cost per credit hour. Create an Excel spreadsheet summarizing your data and charts of student body size and cost per credit hour. Using Word, create a Web page and embed the worksheet on the home page of the Web site. Create another Web page, and embed the charts from Excel. Create a link to the Excel chart Web page and a link to each school's Web page.

3 ◗ Your uncle has requested your assistance in gathering inventory data for his antique shop. Create an Access database and add ten items to it with the following information for each item: item number, category, description, year of origin, purchase price, and sale price. From this table, create a data access page with inquiry capability only, using the category as the group level. Include the item number, description, year or origin, and sale price in the data access page. Use a search engine to find relevant links about each category and create links to one Web page each for each category at the bottom of the data access page.

4 ◗◗ As a member of the Blank Pages Book Club, you have been asked to create an online repository of the members' book collections. Create an Access database and add your own book collection to the database. The included fields should be: owner, fiction/non-fiction, genre, publisher, date published, and author. From this table, create a data access page with inquiry capability only, using the genre as the group level. Create a Web page using Word that will act as the home page for the book club and create a link to the data access page. Be sure to include a link to your e-mail address on the Web page.

5 ◗◗◗ As an investment analyst for Millionaire Investments, you recommend stocks to clients. Choose a stock or other investment and gather information about the company, including information about the investment's past performance. Create an Excel 3-D Bar chart to summarize the financial information that you find. Create a PowerPoint presentation that contains at least four major points regarding this investment that you want to convey to potential investors. Embed the Excel chart into one of the PowerPoint slides. Save the PowerPoint presentation as Web pages. Include relevant links to Web pages regarding the investment.